Sheila,

Sleeping with God:

A Biblical Guide to Christian Meditation

K. D. Weaver

Peace + Blessings

To my enemies, strangers, friends, and family.

To my wife, Lynnette, for believing in Geist.

"And the LORD God caused a deep sleep to fall on Adam, and he slept"

Genesis 2:21

Table of Contents

A Note to the Reader of This Book

Stereotypes and false characterizations have prevented you from an organic religion. You have categorized Christianity as a Western religion even though it was birthed in the Middle East and influenced by a Middle Eastern culture. When you think of Christianity, you think of Europe, Rome, and the Vatican, but Jesus never spent any of his life in those places.

You often associate Christianity with gargantuan cathedrals and elaborate edifices, yet the first century Christians used ordinary homes as their places of worship. Followers of Christ celebrated the Lord's Supper in homes[1]. They preached and taught the Gospel of Jesus Christ[2] and baptized new believers in homes[3].

When you speak of religions that mandate the removal of shoes to enter their sacred places, you name Islam and Buddhism. Yet the removal of shoes was a biblical practice. Moses was told to remove his shoes because he stood on holy ground.[4] The custom during Jesus' time was to remove one's sandals upon entrance into a home and the 1st century Christians worshiped in the home.

When you consider Christian worship, images of pews and sitting in a building come to mind. Yet Jesus, his disciples and the early church were immersed in a culture where the movement of the body was an integral part of worship. When the magi went to visit baby Jesus they "fell to the ground and worshiped Him."[5] Satan promised Jesus worldly glory if he would "fall down and worship [him]."[6] When the mother of James and John came to Jesus with a petition, the scriptures tells us she "came to Jesus with her sons, bowing down and making a request of Him."[7] To prostrate oneself was a part of worship and sign of respect.

Lastly, when you think of meditation you think of Eastern religions and new age movements. Yet Jesus was immersed in a culture that practiced meditation. Meditation is mentioned explicitly and implicitly throughout the Scriptures. The Psalmist wrote of God, "I will meditate on Your precepts and regard Your ways."[8] Meditation was an essential part of incorporating God's Law into one's life. The Gospels often record Jesus' visits to isolated places (deserts, mountains and gardens) to pray and reflect on God's plan and purpose for his life.

Meditation as a Christian practice has been hidden in plain sight for centuries. It is clearly present in the Scriptures. It can be confirmed from various religious and theological traditions. Yet what you need first and foremost is to embrace a return to the way Jesus practiced his faith, a return to Middle Eastern Christianity and specifically, a return to meditation is not Scriptural proof, or religious or theological evidence. What you need is a fresh, spirit filled perspective. What you need is a rebirth in how you view yourself as a person of faith so that God's spirit may be unleashed. Only with your prayers for God's grace can you see. May God grant you the vision to see anew.

Preface

My Catholic school religion teacher mandated that we study all major world religions in addition to Christianity. We dove into Hinduism, Buddhism, Daoism and Islam. I became enthralled by one particular aspect of the Eastern religions: their focus on meditation as a way to commune with the Divine. I began not only reading about various forms of meditation, but also practicing them. I purchased yoga tapes and rehearsed breathing techniques. I remember making a sign which read, "Meditating, do not disturb" and taping it to my bedroom door.

As I entered college and continued to study Eastern religions, I asked myself the questions, "Why can't the Church have this? Why don't Christians meditate?" Once I became a pastor in the Protestant Church, the insignificant place that meditation held became apparent to me again. However, as a minister, the reasons for the absence of meditation in the Church were much clearer to me.

One of the greatest obstacles between the Church and meditation is the Scriptures. Cynthia Bourgeault, a leading author and teacher of the Christian contemplative tradition, writes, "It would make matters hugely simpler, of course, if we could claim any clear, unambiguous scriptural references to substantiate that Jesus either practiced meditation himself or specifically taught it to his disciples. We can't."[9] Bourgeault repeats the belief among many that there is no explicit scriptural support for Christian meditation. Similarly, Peter Toon, author of *From Mind to Heart: Christian Meditation Today*, states, "Yet the modern, Western reader of the four Gospels does not see any obvious references to Jesus actually involved in meditating. Nowhere in any translation of the Greek New Testament do we read 'and Jesus meditated.'"[10] Toon and Bourgeault acknowledge the absence of unequivocal scriptural evidence for Jesus meditating, but make a case that Christian meditation is important and justifiable by Scripture. A case for meditation that is compelling for the Church must have the very evidence that most scholars and practitioners admit is not present.

What if we have been looking at meditation and the Scriptures all wrong? What if meditation is mentioned and encouraged throughout the Scriptures? What if meditation was simply called another name, like the cross was called the tree or people were called sheep or God was called a shepherd or life was called bread? Whenever one word replaces another, that switch is often based on some type of association. People follow God as sheep follow a shepherd. Eternal life sustains us in the spiritual realm as bread does in the physical.

This work proposes that there is a connection between sleep and meditation in the Scriptures. An authentically biblical form of Christian meditation can be developed from certain passages mentioning sleep. One can easily observe that there is a strong physical resemblance between meditation and sleep. Meditation can occur when your eyes are closed and when you are in a relaxed position similar to sleep. Many guides on the practice of meditation caution not to meditate in a completely relaxed position because you might fall asleep. The distance between meditating and sleeping is very short. If you practice meditation regularly, then most likely at one time or another you have drifted off to sleep. I know I have.

The goals of this work are threefold: to initiate, agitate and justify. This book intends to continue to initiate meditation's vital presence in the Church. Certainly this is not the first book to suggest meditation should have a more central role in the Church. However, more work is ahead for advocates for Christian meditation than behind us. Positioning meditation as a staple Christian discipline is still a task that needs to be fulfilled. Two, this work intends to agitate. Hopefully, as a result of reading this book, your conceptions of familiar Bible passages and understanding of meditation will be challenged. By God's grace you will become a little uncomfortable about what you believe and that agitation will lead to a greater Christ-likeness. Last, this work intends to justify that meditation plays a prominent role in the Scriptures and should play a prominent role in the lives of all 21st century disciples of Jesus Christ.

Almost two decades later, I feel more confident than ever in answering the questions that I posed in high school. Yes, Christians do meditate. Yes, the Bible encourages us to do so.

03/13/09

Introduction

What does it mean to "sleep with someone?" The phrase sounds somewhat indecent when first uttered. It conjures up private quarters, darkness and vulnerability. It immediately reminds us of hidden passions and midnight rendezvous. For many, the very images and thoughts associated with the phrase mean that it must be spoken in a whisper.

What does it mean to sleep with God? That question might sound strange to some, but a closer look at the Scriptures can cause us to entertain it. God is often described as the groom and his people as the bride. The covenant of the Law is often depicted as a marriage. So when God and his people come together on their honeymoon night, what do they do?

Sleeping with God is possible. It is a scandalous act. It involves tremendous vulnerability. It is often done in private quarters, in darkness and in the late hours of the night. It is only spoken about in whispers within the Church. It is pleasurable beyond your wildest dreams and sometimes it is called meditation. This book desires to create a scandal in the Church of monumental proportions. This work will encourage everyone in the Church to sleep with God and then gossip about it to each person he or she meets.

Sleep and the Bible

A few words are found predominantly in the Scriptures that can be translated as sleep. The Hebrew words *shakab* and *yashen* are frequently rendered as sleep in the Old Testament. The Hebrew word *tardemah* is commonly translated as "deep sleep." The Greek words *katheudo* and *koimao* are employed most often in the New Testament. The Hebrew and Greek words for sleep have multiple meanings and nuances besides the literal understanding. When commenting on the usage of sleep in the Hebrew Scriptures, Thomas H. McAlpine writes, "References to sleep occur throughout the Old Testament. And these references occur in an apparently wide variety of contexts. Only rarely is sleep itself the topic; in the bulk of cases, sleep is mentioned in connection with some other topic."[1] Sometimes the same word possesses different meanings, which is often seen with *shakab*. Other times, different words used for sleep carry distinct nuances and meanings, as in the case of *katheudo* and *koimao*.[2] One passage that uses a Greek or Hebrew word for sleep could have multiple meanings or implications. Throughout the Bible, sleep signifies many things: sexual relations, divine conduct, spiritual ineptness and death.

Sleep as Sex

Sleep is often used as an analogy for sexual relations. After King Abimelech discovered that Isaac lied about the identity of his wife, the king replied, "What is this you have done to us? One of the men might well have slept with your wife, and you would have brought guilt upon us."[3] Likewise, Exodus 22:16 reads, "If a man seduces a virgin who is not pledged to be married and sleeps with her, he must pay the bride-price, and she shall be his wife." The biblical examples for sleep as sexual relations are prevalent and certainly not foreign to our modern vernacular.

Sleep and God

Throughout the book of Psalms, sleep is used as a way to personify God. Psalm 44:23 states, "Awake, O Lord, Why do you sleep? Rouse yourself; do not reject us forever."[4] Similarly, Psalm 78:65 proclaims, "Then the Lord awoke as from sleep, as a man wakes from the stupor of wine."[5] The psalmist used sleep to characterize the absence of visible divine activity. Yet the application of sleep to God should not lead the reader to imply God's lack of concern. In reference to the care and watchfulness of God, Psalm 121 is clear. "Indeed, he who watches over Israel will neither slumber nor sleep. The Lord watches over you—the Lord is your shade at your right hand."[6] Concerning the Psalms' anthropomorphism of God, Bernard Batto states, "The image of God as never sleeping, like its opposite function in Israel, is an effective expression of her faith in Yahweh as the creator and king whose control over the universe is absolute and eternal."[7] The book of Psalms employed sleep as a way to express contextual attitudes and feelings toward God as well as to make theological statements. Biblical writers applied human characteristics to God in order to understand and relate to God.

Sleep as Spiritual Ineptness

Sleep as spiritual ineptness can be seen in both testaments. The prophet Isaiah proclaims, "The Lord has brought over you a deep sleep: He has sealed your eyes (the prophets); he has covered your heads (the seers). For this whole vision is nothing but words sealed in a scroll."[8] The prophet compares sleep to a lack of spiritual comprehension. While instructing his disciples about the fulfillment of Messianic events, Jesus states,

> No one knows about the day or hour, not even the angels in heaven, nor the Son, but only the Father. Be on guard! Be alert! You do not know when that time will come. It's like a man going away: He leaves his house and puts his

servants in charge, each with his assigned task, and tells the one at the door to keep watch. Therefore, keep watch, because you do not know when the owner of the house will come back—whether in the evening, or at midnight, or when the rooster crows, or at dawn. If he comes suddenly, do not let him find you sleeping. What I say to you, I say to everyone: "Watch!"[9]

In the gospel of Mark, Jesus used sleep as a way to express spiritual inattentiveness. First Thessalonians 5:10 and Ephesians 5:14 arguably employ a similar understanding of sleep.[10]

Sleep as Death

Death is one of the most common understandings for sleep. The psalmist writes, "Look on me and answer, O Lord my God. Give light to my eyes, or I will sleep in death."[11] Psalm 90:5 depicts the power of God and reads, "You sweep men away in the sleep of death; they are like the new grass of the morning."[12] Paul was also familiar with this understanding for sleep. He writes, "Listen, I tell you a mystery: We will not all sleep, but we will all be changed in a flash, in the twinkling of an eye, at the last trumpet. For the trumpet will sound, the dead will be raised imperishable, and we will be changed."[13] The New International Version translation of Matthew 27:52 leaves no room for ambiguity and translates the Greek word *ketheudo*, which is traditionally translated as sleep, as died. The King James Version stays with the more literal rendering: "And the graves were opened: and many bodies of the saints which slept arose."[14] The parallel between sleep and death is frequent in the Scriptures.

4

Sleep as Meditation

Alternative understandings of sleep came about in part because of some similarity and association that sleep had with sex, divine conduct, spiritual ineptness or death. Sleep also has an association with meditation. McAlpine attests to this association in a table he created entitled, "Situations lexically related to sleep."[15] One of the situations he relates to sleep is nocturnal activity, which he defines as "breaking off sleep to praise YHWH, also meditating, lamenting, planning evil (all in bed)."[16] The nocturnal activity of meditation is found throughout the Scriptures. Joshua 1:8 reads, "Do not let this Book of the Law depart from your mouth; meditate on it day and night, so that you may be careful to do everything written in it."[17] Similarly, Psalm 1:1-2 reads, "Blessed is the man who does not walk in the counsel of the wicked or stand in the way of sinners or sit in the seat of mockers. But his delight is in the law of the Lord, and on his law he meditates day and night."[18] Before Isaac met his bride to be, Genesis recounts, "He went out to the field one evening to meditate."[19] In each passage, meditation happens throughout the evening or night, when sleep occurs. The passages imply that one can meditate at night in lieu of sleeping.

The association between meditation and sleep is not only seen in reference to time, but also in reference to location. Psalm 63:6 reads, "On my bed I remember you; I think of you through the watches of the night."[20] Remembering is a vital part of meditation.[21] In reference to God's expectation of Israel, Peter Toon writes,

> Each Saturday they were to meditate on the story of the exodus, using their imagination to picture its details in order to remind them of, and give them a desire to,

observe their covenant with God. Using understanding, memory, and imagination in meditation was more than a once-weekly duty. It was to be a daily exercise.[22]

Toon points out that employing one's memory is an essential part of meditation. For example, if you are meditating on God's goodness, then you must draw instances from your memory where God performs amazing acts and reflect on them. The psalmist remembers God in his bed so he can meditate on God. Psalm 4 implies a particular order in the relationship between sleep and meditation. The Psalm petitions, "Meditate within your heart on your bed and be still."[23] Then the Psalm ends with verse eight, "I will both lie down in peace and sleep, for You alone, O Lord, make me dwell in safety." The Psalmist asks one to go to bed and meditate. After the meditation is over, then the psalmist states that one can sleep. Meditation is the activity that you practice in bed before you sleep.

The Psalms indicate that meditation is to be practiced at the same time and in the same location as sleep. Meditating at night in bed transitioned one into sleep. The monastic tradition preserved this connection between sleep and meditation. One of the earliest Christian monks, St. Anthony, stated, "Pray continually, avoid vainglory, sing psalms before sleep and on awaking; hold in your heart the commandments of Scripture."[24] Likewise when speaking of a particular verse of the Bible, Abbott Isaacs proclaims, "Let sleep come upon you still considering this verse, till having been [molded] by the constant use of it, you grow accustomed to repeat it even in your sleep."[25] Meditation on Scripture before one sleeps was the expectation. The ideal was to meditate on Scriptures during one's sleep and then carry the meditation over to the morning.

The monastic community embodied the mandate to meditate on God's Word day and night, while awake and asleep.

For centuries, Christian mystics have intuitively used the concept of sleep to express contemplation, which is the desired end point of meditation[26]. The anonymous author of *The Cloud of Unknowing* writes in a lesser known work,

> It is not without reason that I liken this work to sleep. For in sleep the natural faculties cease from their work and the whole body takes its full rest, nourishing and renewing itself. Similarly in spiritual sleep, those restless spiritual faculties, Imagination and Reason, are securely bound and utterly emptied. Happy the spirit, then, for it is freed to sleep soundly and rest quietly in loving contemplation of God simply as he is, while the whole inner man is wonderfully nourished and renewed.[27]

Here the author equates spiritual sleep to contemplation (resting in God). The list would be long if one quoted every mystic who used sleep to discuss contemplation. As William Johnston states, "...the comparison of mystical prayer to sleep, the 'naked intent of the will,' the 'chaste and perfect love of God,' 'the sovereign point of the spirit'—all these are pregnant with tradition, [are] used by so many Christian authors..."[28] A range of Christian writers employed this analogy of sleep.

The association between sleep and meditation is even acknowledged today by twenty-first century Christian leaders and writers. When discussing the discipline of memorization, Richard Foster writes, "Then, too, as we submit ourselves to this small discipline, God is able to reach us through the word of Scripture at any given moment, even as we sleep. Memorization is a helpful means to enhance our meditation upon Scripture."[29] The Hebrew Scriptures cultivated a religious association between sleep and meditation. Christian traditions, such as monasticism and mysticism, throughout the centuries maintained this association.

Indications that sleep can be linked with meditation are not limited to the Hebrew Scriptures. The New Testament opens with Joseph, Jesus' father, considering whether he should leave his fiancé, Mary. The Gospel of Matthew proclaims,

> But while he thought on these things, behold, the angel of the Lord appeared unto him in a dream, saying, Joseph, thou son of David, fear not to take unto thee Mary thy wife: for that which is conceived in her is of the Holy Ghost...Then Joseph being raised from sleep did as the angel of the Lord had bidden him, and took unto him his wife.[30]

In the midst of his reflection he transitioned into sleep. In line with the method described in the Psalms, Joseph meditated prior to sleep.

The Gospels reveal that Jesus was well schooled in the Psalms. He quoted from them throughout his ministry. In Christ's greatest moment of agony and suffering, he cried out words from the Psalms, "My God, My God, why have You forsaken Me?"[31] Jesus wove the Psalms into his heart so tightly that he used them to express his most basic emotions and calls of distress. When we are distressed we cry out the words which are second nature to us. In a moment of crisis we instinctively cry out "help". Jesus' instinct was to cry out the Psalms.

If Jesus knew the Psalms (which he did), he knew of meditation. If Jesus followed the Psalms (which he did), he practiced meditation. Meditation on Scripture, God's creation and works would have been a part of Jesus' routine. Before Jesus went to sleep, he meditated. When he arose early in the morning, he meditated. With this foreknowledge passages that mention Jesus praying in the evening hold a new significance.

The Gospel of John proclaims, "[Jesus] departed again to the mountain by Himself alone. Now when evening came, His disciples went down to the sea, got into the boat, and went over the sea toward Capernaum. And it was already dark, and Jesus had not come to them."[32] Evening comes and Jesus begins to do what he routinely does at night: meditate and pray in a solitary place. Jesus' devotional life eventually moved his disciples to want to learn these disciplines.[33]

Jesus taught his disciples how to pray with the utterance of the Lord's Prayer. The prayer that Jesus gives his disciples assumes that meditation already has taken place. The Lord's Prayer cannot be said meaningfully without meditation. We must reflect upon God's will before we can pray for it to come. We must reflect upon our sins before we can ask God to forgive them. We must reflect upon the trespasses that others have committed against us before we can sincerely forgive others. The Lord's Prayer is given in the context of routine meditation. Jesus taught his disciples how to meditate with his actions. He constantly went to solitary places to reflect upon God's will for his life and the disciples noticed this practice. Eventually, Jesus invites a few disciples to private meditation and prayer sessions with him and these disciples on more than one occasion fall asleep during them.[34] Could it be the disciples slept because Jesus (at least sometimes) was asking them to meditate and pray at times that they were accustomed to being asleep?

Various biblical accounts indicate a connection between sleep and meditation. More importantly, I propose that the present day Christian community can benefit greatly from making these connections.

Sleep as Negative Meditation

The Bible does not always view sleep as a desirable state. The book of Proverbs contains some of the most explicit sentiments against sleep. Proverbs 10:5 states, "He who sleeps during the harvest is a disgraceful son."[35] Proverbs 19:15 reads, "Laziness brings on deep sleep"[36] and 20:13 proclaims, "Do not love sleep or you will grow poor; stay awake and you will have food to spare."[37] These verses are not suggesting that sleep is bad, but they point out that too much sleep or sleeping at the wrong times will lead to harsher circumstances.

The message of Proverbs is straightforward. The more you sleep, the less time you have to work. The less time you have to work, the less chance you have to create a productive and prosperous life. Yet these proverbs provide another message when we view sleep in a broader sense. Just as sleep is not always a desirable state, neither are various forms of meditation. That statement sounds strange, doesn't it? How can meditation be bad, unhealthy or even destructive for us? Meditation is spiritual. It is peaceful. It is supposed to be a good thing, right?

Meditation is not just something you choose to do in a quiet room; it is also an activity that you sometimes do unintentionally in your everyday routine. Thomas Merton, a Benedictine monk, defined meditation in his book *Spiritual Direction and Meditation*. He wrote, "To meditate is to exercise the mind in serious reflection. This is the broadest sense of the

10

word 'meditation.' The term in this sense is not confined to religious reflection."[38] Merton is clear to point out that by definition meditation is not necessarily a religious activity. Walter Kaiser is even more explicit in his identification of negative meditation. He writes, "Some meditation can be harmful."[39] The Psalms attest to the possible nefarious side of meditation. Psalm 19:14 states, "Let the words of my mouth and the meditation of my heart Be acceptable in your sight…"[40] The Psalmist's petition that his meditation be acceptable implies that some meditations are unacceptable to God. Likewise Psalm 104:34 states, "May my meditation be sweet to Him."[41] The Psalmist's request that his meditation be sweet implies that some meditations can be sour to God. A constant diet of television and movies can place you in a meditative state of lust, perpetually reflecting on sexual images. A steady regimen of video games and visual stimulation can place you in a meditative state of violence, in which you crave and ponder the excitement of combat in whatever form it presents itself. The repetitive motion of eating snack foods can place you in a meditative state of hunger or sensory stimulation. The bombardment of musical notes and lyrics can also place you in a meditative state. The list can continue. You are constantly meditating, whether you are religious or not, spiritual or not, or even desire to meditate or not, and all forms of meditation are not healthy.

Just as various biblical accounts concerning sleep can offer insight into the practice of meditation, accounts concerning waking up can offer insight into the practice of reverse meditation, which bring us out of destructive meditative states.

Summary of the Book

The following chapters will offer some insight into particular ways to sleep and awake with God. This book is organized into three sections. Section 1, *A Time to Sleep*, offers guidance on types of meditation that foster healthy relationships, divine insight, inner peace, and moral consciousness. An analysis of Adam and Abram's encounters with sleep in Genesis is provided. Jesus' sleep throughout a storm in the gospel of Mark and the moral dimension of Uriah's sleep in 2nd Samuel is examined. Each chapter in Section 1 is organized into three main parts: the goal, premeditation, and meditation. The goal exposes the purpose of the meditation. The premeditation part highlights the conditions that set the stage for the meditation to occur. The meditation part reveals the process that you must undertake to sleep with God.

Section 2, *A Time to Awake*, explores negative meditative states, as well as the counter-meditative practices which can break those states. Meditative practices that help counter apathy, church fatigue, escapism, and fatalism are explored. Jesus' experience with Jairus' sleeping daughter, Eutychus dozing off in church and Jonah's nap on a boat are examined. Peter's sleep in jail is also explored. Each chapter in Section 2 is organized into three main parts: the goal, negative meditation, and reverse meditation. The goal reveals the purpose for the reverse meditation. The negative meditation part exposes the crucial steps that lead a person into a harmful meditative state. The reverse meditation part takes the reader through the process, which will lead a person out of the harmful state.

Each chapter in Sections 1 and 2 ends with a prayer, reflection questions and an activity to help you use the meditation in your everyday life. A meditation verse, which can be repeated during the meditation, accompanies each activity.

The last section, *Sleepiness*, contains three brief looks at the negative meditative states that various biblical characters were not able to "awaken from." This section provides an examination of Samson's sleeping patterns with Delilah, the disciples' sleep in the garden of Gethsemane and Saul's sleep during David's invasion of Saul's camp. The detrimental aspects of meditating on your strengths, self-gratification and your will are outlined. The last section is informative rather than instructional. Hopefully, through the reading and practice of these three sections, you will be inspired to sleep and awake with God.

Chapter 1
Missing Rib Meditation

Genesis 2:15-25

Any discussion of the creation story found in Genesis can lead one into a polarized debate. Are you a creationist or an evolutionist? Do you believe the world was created in six days or millions of years? Do you read the Bible literally or allegorically? Are you on the side of religion or science? What do you think about intelligent design theory? Should it be taught in school? To even mention the creation story of Genesis automatically leads many into thoughts, theories, opinions and speculations about the origin of the world.

Discussion concerning the beginning of the universe can be very stimulating when done in a respectful and loving way. However, to limit the creation story of Genesis to a discussion about the origin of the world does a grave injustice to Christians and non-Christians who read the Bible. The creation story involves so much more than cosmology. It highlights aspects of stewardship. It carries certain dietary implications for us. It comments on the struggle between light and darkness, good and evil, and order and chaos. In addition, the creation story also offers insight about meditation. Particularly, it informs us about a type of meditation that impacts our relationships.

If we could find a word that pulled together the essence of our faith, one word we could use is relationships. If we were to examine our faith tradition, we would find that most of the issues deal with relationships. For example, if we were to look at the Ten Commandments, we would find that at the heart of them are commandments about relationships. "Honor your father and mother" refers to the relationship that you should have towards your parents. "You shall not commit adultery," or put positively, "be faithful to your spouse," refers to the relationship that you should have with your partner. "You shall not lie against your neighbor," and "you shall not covet your neighbor's possessions," refer to the relationship that you should have with the people in your community.

When Jesus was asked to reveal the greatest command, he replied, "Love the Lord your God with all your heart and with all your soul and with all your mind. This is the first and greatest commandment."[1] Jesus was saying to the Pharisees that the greatest command was to be in a proper relationship with God. Throughout the Bible we find that divine judgment is always preceded by people entering into improper relationships with other people or things. One could even say sin is the result of improper relationships.

The Goal

When we turn to the creation story of the Bible, the issue of relationships is also present. God tells Adam that "it is not good (*tob*)"[2] for him to be without companionship. The Hebrew word *tob* suggests a notion of completeness.[3] Hence the phrase "it is good" (or it is complete) is used following God's acts of creation. To say that "it is not good" for Adam to be alone indicates Adam is not whole if he is alone. Once the incompleteness of Adam is identified, then the resolution is provided. God promises to create a companion for Adam. With this promise, the goal of Missing Rib Meditation emerges: to cultivate relationships that are conducive to your wholeness.

People often think of meditation as an activity that propels them to separate from others in a quiet place so they can draw closer to God or have more inner peace. This is the case for some types of meditation. Yet with this form of meditation, the goal is to draw closer to others by allowing God's Spirit to be the "match maker."

If some are able to avoid the theological pitfall that reduces the creation story simply to a cosmological occurrence, then they often fall into a second pitfall. Many would like to reduce the creation story (particularly the parts referring to Adam and Eve) to a discussion over the relationship between the sexes. Similar to those who have a cosmological predisposition, those who identify the primary issue in the creation story as one concerning heterosexuality, miss the texture of the Scriptures.

Adam can be understood as mankind or humanity. If we understand man (*adam*) to mean humanity in Genesis 2:18, then the text becomes a commentary on the social nature of human beings. From this perspective the text tells us that humans are social beings and are not made to be outside of community.

What if we took man (*adam*) in Genesis 2:18 to mean husband? When most people think of the word husband, they think of a male. The origins of the word are associated with the position of a manager or master of a household.[4] The essence of this word is still intact today. A husband is not a male, a husband is a position that a male assumes. In Genesis, Adam held the position of the manager of God's garden. If we understand man (*adam*) to mean husband in Genesis 2:18, then the text becomes a commentary on the need all have for assistance. We are all capable of managing something, but God teaches us that we can accomplish more and with greater excellence when we work with others. We are able to go further when we help others and others help us.

Foremost, we should put aside the notion of sexuality when we read Genesis 2:18 based on Christological considerations. Galatians 3:28 states, "There is neither Jew nor Greek, slave nor free, male nor female, for you are all one in Christ Jesus."[5] What would happen if we read the creation story as if there is neither male nor female but all being the same through Christ? I am not suggesting that we give no consideration to understanding man and woman in the creation story as biologically compatible beings. I do propose that to focus exclusively on the biological aspect causes us to miss the many insights that the creation story can offer us about relationships. Now that we have acknowledged the dynamic nature of relationships, which the creation story reveals, let us examine how the story exposes our need for relationships and how to enter into them properly.

Premeditation

Before God promised Adam a companion, we cannot overlook one important fact: Adam was fulfilling a God-given purpose. God placed Adam in the garden so that he could cater to it, then God told Adam to not eat from a specific tree. Adam was aware of his divine task and he fulfilled his task in the boundaries God established. We will see throughout this book that alignment with one's God-given purpose is an essential component to Christian meditation.

To find the person or persons God has for you without first some awareness of the person God desires you to be is difficult. Part of who God desires you to be involves what tasks God has for you. Those who are unaware of the role God desires for them or who refuse to live out their role within the boundaries God sets will experience a substantial obstacle in the practice of Missing Rib Meditation.

The verses following God's promise to make a companion for Adam can seem strange at first glance. God presented animals before Adam as possible companions! After all the animals are offered to Adam, verse 20 reads, "But for Adam no suitable helper was found."[6] The more you begin to think about this passage, the less odd it will appear. Who is considered man's best friend? It is not a spouse or a next door neighbor, but a canine.

I had a neighbor who called me numerous times in one day and left several messages. When I finally got home and received her messages, I immediately called her back, assuming that she was in a dire state. Well, she was in a horrible state. Her bird had died and she was too emotional to take it out of the cage herself. Anyone who has ever had a pet knows that deep bonds of companionship can be formed with animals (that sometimes even surpass ones we have with humans). Companionship with animals seems less odd when we remember that both humans and animals fall under the umbrella of God's creation. We are all God's creatures. God's presentation did not only provide Adam with options for companionship; it also provided vital lessons about companionship.

Three groups of animals were presented to Adam: livestock, birds of the air, and beasts of the field. Each group possessed certain characterizations among the Hebrew people and their descendants.

Livestock

The livestock or herds were used for labor and as meat for offerings. Livestock and herds were also measures of one's wealth. There was tangible, pragmatic value in having livestock. When God offered Adam the option of having livestock as companions, God wanted to see if Adam would choose a relationship based on material gain.

Many people enter into relationships because of the financial security and stability that can be obtained from them. These people measure and analyze all the benefits that can be captured by being with someone: a nice house, a safe neighborhood, a large bank account, connections to an influential family, or status. God presented Adam with a relationship of leisure and comfort.

Birds of the Air

The birds of the air had a peculiar place among the biblical writers. Objects of the sky were a potential threat to the religion of Yahweh because they were sometimes worshipped (maybe for their proximity to the heavens). Deuteronomy 4:19 warns the Israelites, "And when you look up to the sky and see the sun, the moon and the stars—all the heavenly array—do not be enticed into bowing down to them and worshipping things the Lord your God has apportioned to all the nations under heaven."[7] Many Israelite kings were noted as turning away from God and worshipping the celestial bodies.

The space directly above the Earth did not lose its hazardous aspects in the New Testament. Satan is depicted as "ruler of the kingdom of air."[8] The realm above the Earth and those objects that filled it always held the potential to sway people away from God. When God presented the birds of the air to Adam, God was placing relationships in front of him that could distract him from his sole commitment to God. Some may have experienced this type of relationship. The person is so dynamic, so beautiful, so smart, so appealing, or so whatever that makes you stop in your tracks, that you become in awe of him or her. A relationship based on veneration is easier to fall into than many of us realize. There is nothing wrong with loving a person and being excited about being with him or her. Yet sometimes our involvement with a person can become a distraction to our ONE and only God. Adam was offered a relationship that could rival his relationship with God.

Beasts of the Field

The last category of God's creation that was presented before Adam was the beasts of the field. The field was often associated with a place that was isolated and believed to be outside the view of others. Cain took his brother Abel to the field to kill him because he thought no one was looking (not even God).[9] Joseph's brothers plotted to slay Joseph in the field where no one would know what happened.[10] Jesse's youngest son, David, was out in the fields tending to the flock while his brothers were being considered for the kingship of Israel.[11] Jesse allowed David to stay in the fields because he never thought his youngest son would be considered by the prophet Samuel. After Judas had realized the gravity of his act, he went out into the field to take his own life.[12] The field was often the place where people believed no one could see or cared what was happening.

When God presented the beasts of the field to Adam, he was presenting relationships to him that would lead him to commit and hide ungodly acts. Many of us, at one time or another in our lives, have had companionships that made us feel "free" from righteous conduct. In the contexts of these relationships, we say to ourselves, "Nobody will know." "They don't know my church friends." "They don't know my family." "They don't know the people that I work with." "They don't know my neighbors." "They won't tell anyone." "I can let loose around them and do what I want around them, because they don't know all my associates and contacts." Being authentic around a group of people is fine, but using a group of people or a person as a blanket to engage in ungodly behavior is unacceptable. Adam chose not to enter into relationships that would make him feel outside the view of God's expectations and judgment.

Through God's display of these various creatures to Adam, Adam was tested with inappropriate companionships and had the insight to acknowledge that they were incompatible. If you are receptive you can learn great lessons about who you are compatible with from people with whom you are incompatible and from relationships that did not go well. You will have greater difficulty embracing the benefits of Missing Rib Meditation if you are in the midst of unhealthy relationships and unable to recognize their harmfulness.

You must let go of your former conceptions of relationships to become ready to receive a type of relationship beyond your imagination, which brings wholeness and greater intimacy with God. You must even let go of some your conceptions of good relationships before God can show you what a good (*tob*) relationship is.

Meditation

God put Adam to sleep while Adam was reflecting upon who would be a suitable companion for him. While Adam was in this state, God took a part from Adam's side (traditionally portrayed as Adam's rib) and then sealed his body. God put Adam to sleep so that he could remove something from him and used the piece from Adam to create a companion for him. Adam experienced a loss that would lead to true companionship and wholeness. What Adam lost led to his completion. *Missing Rib Meditation involves reflection on what you should be releasing to others so that life can emerge.* Missing Rib Meditation seeks what you should surrender because by releasing it, life can be sustained and created.

I discovered the power of Missing Rib Meditation when I became a kidney donor to my father. After my father had spent several years recovering from a massive stroke and rehabilitating his body, he faced a new challenge. The years of hypertension had damaged his kidney and forced him to begin dialysis, a bi-weekly procedure to cleanse the toxins from his blood. The doctors placed my father on a donor list and family members started to get screened to become kidney donors. As soon as the members of my family began their medical evaluations, I felt that I was going to be the one to donate the kidney. A steady, soft sentiment lingered with me that I was the one. When I eventually did get tested for compatibility, the doctors found I was an almost perfect match with my father (a 4 out of 5 match to be exact). I experienced a turbulent surgery and rocky recovery, but my father sailed through the procedure beautifully and his health soared afterwards.

That experience (both before and after the surgery) led me to a simple revelation. What is taken from you can be used to produce life. What was taken from me enabled my father to have a new life and better quality of life. But what was taken from me also enabled me to have a new life. After the surgery I was able to have a new relationship with my father. We shared a trying, unforgettable experience. In a literal sense, we had become one. So much life came out of the kidney I lost.

Relationship Between Loss and Gain

One of the most paradoxical messages that Jesus reiterated throughout his ministry was this relationship between loss and gain. Jesus proclaimed, "For whoever wants to save his life will lose it, but whoever loses his life for me will find it."[13] Jesus spoke these words to his disciples to explain the necessity of his death. The disciples and Peter specifically could not grasp why Jesus had to suffer, be rejected and die. They did not understand how anything good could come from the loss of his reputation, body, ministry, and life. When Peter scolded Jesus for even the thought of such a devastating loss, Jesus responded, "Get behind me, Satan! You are a stumbling block to me; you do not have in mind the things of God, but the things of men."[14] To treat loss as something that must be avoided at all costs is a worldly mindset incompatible with the kingdom of God that Jesus brings forth.

Jesus' Notion of Completion

In loss there is life, gain and even abundance. This message is not only evident in the lessons and sermons that Jesus proclaimed, but also in his interactions with those both inside and on the outskirts of the Jewish faith. Jesus' encounter with the rich young ruler in the gospels is a prime example of the message of loss and gain. The gospel of Matthew depicts the young ruler as someone who had not only knowledge of the Law, but lived in compliance with it. He was a religious, good and moral person by most peoples' standards. Yet this man felt that something was missing in his life. He felt that there was still a void present in the midst of all his accomplishments, status and righteousness. The young man uttered, "What do I still lack?"[15] Jesus response was simple, "If you want to be perfect, go, sell your possessions and give to the poor, and you will have treasure in heaven. Then come, follow me."[16] The Greek word *teleios* for perfect does not mean without flaw but implies a notion of completion or fulfillment. Jesus told the young ruler if he wanted to fill his void, then he must give up his possessions. One of the first steps to fulfillment for Jesus was to let something go.

This message seems so counter intuitive to us because we are told the exact opposite almost every second of our lives. We turn on the television and see commercials that offer products that will make us more beautiful, healthy, happy, smart, popular or more complete if only we buy them. Fulfillment is offered to us every second of every day by the world. It always comes in the form of a new car, house, gadget, relationship, book, movie, pair of shoes, suit or some other type of acquisition.

Loss is crucial to the notion of completion that Jesus brought because loss allows us to have greater access to Christ. Notice that Jesus told the young ruler to release his possessions and then he could follow him. The release had to occur before the following. Jesus said that, "Small is the gate and narrow is the road that leads to life, and only a few find it."[17] When you are walking through a small gate you cannot get through the gate with a lot of stuff. You must put the stuff down in order to enter. If you have built an identity around your stuff, then to put down your possession is like letting go of who you are, which is frightening for most. This young ruler's possession had become a part of his identity. So when Jesus asked him to surrender his possession, the man could have felt as if he was losing himself. But the loss of himself is exactly what he needed to experience to find himself in Christ.

The relationship between loss and gain is also seen in Jesus' encounter with Zacchaeus. Zacchaeus was a chief tax collector. His profession was to collect things and his reputation was that he collected over and beyond what he was entitled. Zacchaeus was, in a literal sense, living a life that was the antithesis to Jesus' new message of completion. After Jesus invited himself to be a guest at Zacchaeus' house and Zacchaeus vowed to give at least fifty percent of his possessions to the needy, Jesus proclaimed, "Today salvation has come to his house."[18] Salvation comes after Zacchaeus pledges to let go of something.

Jesus offers us a more accurate understanding of completion than we could ever find in our modern world. We experience so much self-induced sadness, pain and suffering because we have the wrong notion in mind. We believe that the way we become complete is by obtaining more. We believe that if we just had more insight, more schooling, more money, more contacts, more power, more status, more stuff, then we could be complete. But completion comes from loss, not gain. Wholeness comes from sacrifice, not accumulation.

We go in the opposite direction from being complete and having healthy relationships when we fear losing something that we possess (either material or immaterial). Completion comes through the releasing of yourself. Missing Rib

26

Meditation is not simply focusing on what you need to surrender, it is also releasing those things. You are practicing Missing Rib Meditation when you let go without hesitation and almost unconsciously of those things that will prevent holistic and God-centered connections with others.

Missing Rib Meditation Distinctiveness

A few aspects of Adam's sleep are drastically different from the common notion of meditation. Foremost, God caused the sleep to occur. Kosuke Koyama, in his article, "Adam in Deep Sleep", believes that whether or not one acknowledges God as the initiator of Adam's sleep has a profound impact on one's worldview. He writes,

> There are two major living outlooks current in our world today. One looks at the universe remembering that Adam was asleep at one critical moment in the story of creation, and that signifies that he cannot establish his own self-identity and his place in the cosmos unless he makes important reference to the One who put him into the "deep sleep."...The other viewpoint looks at the universe with the understanding that Adam has no such "transcendental sleep." He is therefore the center of all things and he named all things. If Adam did sleep, it was caused by himself, not by God.[19]

For Koyama to acknowledge God as the cause of Adam's sleep is to acknowledge that humanity cannot know the world or even know himself or herself without the Divine. Yet to disregard that Adam's sleep was initiated by God, reflects a viewpoint of human independence and self power. One's acknowledgment of God as the cause of Adam's sleep also has monumental implications for one's conception of meditation.

When most of us think of meditation, we think of a state that we can initiate and stop at our will. God initiating Adam's deep sleep shatters that notion. It puts God's grace and will inescapably in meditation.

One reason meditation has been shunned or ignored by so many Christians is because of the rigid individualism and autonomy associated with it. If *I* sit here long enough, if *I* focus hard enough and *I* am quiet enough, *I* can achieve inner peace. *I* can unite with the Divine. Many conceptions of meditation remind me of the story of the Tower of Babel. The people believed that they could reach heaven with or without God's consent. Any activity that does not need or desire God's grace and God's will should be troubling to us as people of faith. A biblically grounded conception of meditation is more similar to Jacob's Ladder. God provides the means for our ascension. He reaches down to us and allows us to come closer.

I am certainly not proposing that all meditation requires God's active intervention or that God must cause us to meditate. However, I would propose that certain depths of meditation cannot be experienced without God's consent and causation. Remember, Adam did not only sleep, but the text tells us that he was put into a deep sleep *(tardemah)*.

Conclusion

The differences between the first Adam and the second Adam—Jesus—are often highlighted. The frequently-cited fifth chapter of Romans contrasts the trespass and death associated with Adam with the gift and life associated with Jesus. Adam could be perceived in some regards as the antithesis of Jesus. Although the differences between Adam and Jesus are vital to

Christian theology, the similarities between the two are also worthy of attention.

Adam was a gardener in Eden. Mary mistook Jesus for a gardener when she went to mourn over his body. Adam had a rib taken from his side. Jesus was pierced in his side while on the cross. The rib that Adam lost led to his completion. The life that Jesus lost led to the restoration of humanity. I would propose that Jesus practiced Missing Rib Meditation because he reflected on how his loss would lead to life.[20] He released his life so that we could have life.

Prayer

Ever-sufficient God, may I become less so that you can use me more. Where selfishness and fear abide, cast them out. Allow all that I release to lead to my wholeness. In my sacrifice and lack, may life emerge. Amen.

How to Sleep with God

Review

Goal: Cultivate relationships that lead to wholeness.

Premeditation: Gain the ability to identify an unhealthy relationship.

Meditation: Reflect on what you should release so life and wholeness can emerge.

Reflection

1) Can you remember an instance when letting go or giving up something made you feel better? What led you to do it?

2) Make a timeline which reflects your responsibilities, activities, leisure time, etc. for tomorrow.

3) Analyze the timeline above. What could you release, surrender or give away (material or immaterial) tomorrow that may lead to greater wholeness in your relationships, community or world?

Activity

Pick one thing that you will let go of tomorrow and then write it down on a sheet of paper. Sit down, close your eyes and imagine how you will let go of that thing tomorrow. After you have imagined your release, memorize the meditation verse below.

Repeat your verse throughout the next day. At the end of the day look at your paper and determine if you have released it. If not, keep it for tomorrow and repeat the same activity.

Meditation Verse

"Into your hands"[1]

Post-Meditation Questions

1) Did you tend to release things that were material or immaterial?

2) Did you tend to focus on any particular relationships and avoid others? Why?

3) Did you notice any differences in your relationships?

4) Did you notice any differences in yourself while practicing this meditation?

Chapter 2
Seer Meditation

Genesis 15:7-18

As a minister, I am fascinated by people who are indifferent to or disgusted with the Church and Christian faith. Why do they view it as unimportant? Why do they have so much resentment towards it? A common response I hear is, "I don't need to go to church to worship God. I can read my Bible and praise God in my house." This response turns the Christian faith into a self-serve buffet line and negates the necessity of Christian fellowship to become the Body of Christ.

Another classic response is, "Organized religion is too restrictive for me. I am more into spirituality." When did religion become separated from spirituality? I missed that memo. Jesus told a Pharisee named Nicodemus that he must be born of water and the Spirit. Then come the blatant attacks. "The church is full of hypocrites." "That church takes up too many collections." Yet there is one question that prevents even this Christian minister from an automatic rebuttal: "How do you know?" What makes this question so unique is that it is shared by Christians. Even Christians would like to have more certainty, more assurance, specific details, and evidence to show them that being a disciple of Christ is worth the effort.

Most Christians know the power of coming together to worship. They know and have experienced spirituality through the Christian faith. They know about or participate in the service that the Church provides to the local community and larger world. Yet all Christians have asked at one time or another, "How am I to know what God is calling me to do?"

"How am I going to do what God is calling me to do?" "How is God going to lead me out of this mess?" "How is God going to provide for me here?" "How is this illness which has plagued me for years going to vanish?" "How is this heartbreak going to heal?" "How will this promotion come my way?" "How is this disobedient child going to turn around?" "How will I ever find my help mate?" "How is the Lord going to make his presence undeniably visible in my life?"

Yes, even armed with the power of the Holy Scriptures and prayer, we still ask the question "How can we know for sure?" The classic Christian rebuttal—"You have to have faith"—seems so weak (sometimes even when offered to Christians). In an age where we can know so much, we have a difficult time accepting not knowing how God is going to operate in our lives.

The mystery of God pushes us to new depths of faith in God's power and knowledge. I am a personal witness to how God can make a way out of no way (that I am able to see). Although this mystery can be an opportunity to strengthen our faith, we still serve a God of revelation. We serve a God that shines light upon us and places light in us. We serve a God that calls us out of darkness. In short, we also serve a God that desires for us to know more than before we were in a relationship with him. So, when we are asked if there is ever a time when God wants us to know how he operates, we can confidently answer yes.

We certainly have biblical proof. Moses pleaded with God to make his ways more clear so he could serve God more effectively.[1] God allowed Elisha and his servant to witness an invisible army, which surrounded them.[2] Saul doubted that Jesus was the Messiah and Jesus appeared to him on the road to Damascus.[3] Jesus made himself known to Mary after his death.[4] Yes, we serve a God of mystery, a God whose ways and thoughts are higher than our own. Yet we also serve a God who has revealed God's self to humanity time and time again. We also serve a God of revelation.

God's revelation is distinct from man's information. I often stress this distinction each time I lead a Bible class. In every Bible class there is always (at least) one person who is armed with the latest commentary, an article from the web or a historical perspective from a documentary. He or she tries to use the information to solve or understand the issues we are examining in class. Yet his or her intention is incompatible with the goal of Bible class for people of faith, which is to know God more fully.

There are aspects of God that you cannot understand until God makes them known to you, until God reveals them. God's grace is a necessary component to understanding God. Biblical scholarship, historical, social and literary disciplines can help facilitate our understanding of the Bible, but they will never replace God's revelation. That is why, as Christians, we do not simply study the Scriptures, but we pray to God for understanding. We fast while reading the Scriptures. We meditate on the Scriptures. We chant and sing the Scriptures. All as a way of saying, "We know we cannot get this on our own, please help us Lord."

If a book represents the information that allows you to know more, then the light that permits you to read the pages represents revelation. The book is completely useless without the light. Christ is our light and by him we are able to see.

The Goal

When we acknowledge all the times God reveals his ways and thoughts and remember that Christ illuminates our life, Abram's question—how can I know?—seems less audacious. Abram wanted a piece of the action, if you will. He had received a promise from God, but he wanted to know how this promise was going to be fulfilled. To perceive Abram's sentiment as doubt would be inaccurate. The text states, Abram believed that the Lord would fulfill his promise.[5] Abram wanted clarification on how the promise would unfold.

Christians frequently make the distinction between belief and doubt. Yet many studies have shown that the majority of Americans believe in God. So, a distinction between belief in God and doubt of God's existence does not capture the tension many people face. The tension of many concerns a belief in God and how to find the best way to express that belief. Confusion over how to acknowledge God in a religiously diverse world is the primary issue for most. Similar to many believers today, Abram did not doubt God. He was confused about how God would reconcile the promise he received with his current circumstances.

Abram's posture to God is akin to the father who asked Jesus to cast out a demon from his son. Once Jesus said that a healing was possible with the father's belief, the father responded, "I do believe; help me overcome my unbelief!"[6] I do not interpret the father to mean he believes, but he wants to get rid of his doubt. To believe and to doubt at the same time is impossible. I interpret the father to mean that he believed a healing could happen, but could not see or understand how it could. Like Abram, this father had belief, but he wanted insight into how what he believed would occur.

Abram was in a state of flux. He had left his homeland, but had yet to receive a new land. He left his extended family, but had yet to have his first child. He surrendered the comfort and stability of his past life, but obtained no present security.

People of faith can easily relate to Abram. There are times when God moves you to comfort others even when you have yet to secure internal peace. There are moments when God urges you to make financial sacrifices for his Kingdom even before you reach a state of financial abundance. There are moments when God propels you to leave a secure place even when success in your next destination seems uncertain. There are moments when God convicts you to exit a relationship even when future companions are nowhere in sight.

All of us have experienced the feeling of being in flux. When we have taken a few steps out of our past, but have yet to walk into the future promises of God, we hunger for any assurance. We cannot control whether we will receive confirmation from God, but we can make ourselves more receptive to notice God's confirmation if it comes. Seer Meditation helps us with our receptiveness to God.

Seers were people in Israel who received visions and insights concerning the present and future circumstances of God's people. Samuel was the most well-known seer in the Bible. A seer could see clearly what others could not see at all. The goal of Seer Meditation is to become more open to God and more aware of what God desires you to "see."

Premeditation

Put yourself in Abram's shoes for a moment. You asked God a straightforward question and God's immediate response was "Bring me a heifer, a goat and a ram, each three years old, along with a dove and a young pigeon."⁷ Huh? What in the world does that have to do with my question? Abram asked God a question. God responded to the question by commanding him to prepare a sacrifice. For the Israelite culture, the most common form of worship was offering a sacrifice to Yahweh. So, Yahweh responded to Abram's request for certainty with a command to worship.

Worship

Yahweh asked Abram not simply to worship, but to worship before he received his promise. God wanted to see if Abram could worship when he had nothing. If you cannot worship God before you walk into God's promises, then you are less likely to worship God once you have received them. God wants to see if you can worship when you are empty or full, during famine or feast, and in the midst of joy or sadness. God wants to see if you love him or if you love what he can do for you.

Many of the pastors with whom I speak comment that they notice a correlation between status and income and a passion for worship. They believe in many instances, once a person has arrived (in whatever way he or she defines it), his or her worship of God becomes more lackluster. The demands of the job now take precedent. The toys that he or she has worked so hard to obtain must be enjoyed. The money that he or she has acquired must be protected and used with caution. These people allow their abundance to become a distraction to their worship of God. However, those people who have arrived are no worse than those who allow their lack to become a distraction to their worship of God. Some people need more money, rest, time and help, so they feel that they must give

God less. Many times 'the haves' and 'the have nots' share a similar tendency; neither make worship an essential part of their lives.

You asked God for some confirmation about your relationships, finances, career, school, family or about your health and you believed you never received an answer. But God already responded to you. God's response was this: Worship and praise me. Do you want to know God better? Do you want to have clear discernment about where your life is heading? Then you must learn how to worship God.

Worship is not simply coming to church on Sunday, singing a few hymns, reading a few scriptures and listening to a sermon. Worship is a way of life. First Corinthians 10:31 states, "Whether you eat or drink or whatever you do, do it for God's glory."[8] It is something that we can engage in every second of our lives. Worship is using what God has given us according to his will. When we worship, we set the stage for God's revelation to emerge.

There is an interesting relationship between using God-given talents for God (i.e., worship) and greater clarity. When you are able to use God-given talents in an unhindered way, everything seems clear and peaceful in those moments. The laws of time and space are suspended. Everything but the execution of your talent fades into the background. When a singer is singing, when a dancer is dancing, when a preacher is preaching, when an author is writing, when an athlete is playing, when an architect is designing or when a painter is creating, there is no confusion or uncertainty present. They are doing what they are designed to do. Even if everything else in their life is in disarray — their relationships, social skills, health, etc. — they can at least find clarity and rest using their God-given talents. Worship has a way of clearing your heart and mind so you are able to receive the insight God has for you. Worship is the vital condition for Seer Meditation.

Distractions to Worship

Abram made the sacrifices to the Lord, but while he worshipped, some scavenger animals attempted to steal the sacrifices he offered to God. Abram spent time warding off these animals. Forces entered Abram's life that tried to disrupt his worship.

When you possess a grasp of your God-given talents and begin to use them for God's glory, expect people to enter your life and try to derail you. Expect comments like, "You don't make any money doing that." Expect thoughts to pop up in your consciousness like, "Am I really making a difference?" Expect to feel like many of your friends are doing so well and you are struggling. When you adopt a lifestyle of worship, expect that lifestyle to be attacked from mental, emotional, physical and spiritual perspectives.

All forms of worship can lend themselves to routines and habits. Sometimes routines and habits can be practiced while losing the original intention and passion behind them. Authentic worship is an essential condition for Seer Meditation; therefore, continual revivals and reminders of the significance and purpose for worship are important.

Meditation

Abram asked God for insight. God told Abram to make an offering to him. He followed God's order. Abram falls asleep while he tries to figure out how God could fulfill his promises.

A deep sleep falls upon Abram while he meditates on God's promises.

Abram was obedient to all that God commanded him to do and nothing happened. Abram's deep sleep (*tardemah*) in the midst of "nothingness" reveals the core of Seer Meditation. Abram slept when nothing seemed to be happening and no confirmation to his request seemed to be forthcoming.

You have been faithful to what God has called you to do. You are steadfast in going to church throughout the week and tithing your salary. You have tried to bring your children up in the church. You have constantly tried to get and keep your spouse active in church. You may have even changed your career. You have done all that you believe God wants you to do and still nothing is happening. Your church does not acknowledge all that you do. Your finances are still strained. Your children have strayed from the church. Your marriage is in jeopardy. Your health is failing. Your pursuits in ministry are not producing the fruits that you thought they would. You have worshipped God as He commanded and still nothing of benefit occurred.

In those moments, you can become so tempted to give up, try something else or go in a different direction. But those are the moments when you need to be still and wait on the Lord. Those are the moments when you need to sleep. *Seer Meditation involves stilling yourself (and allowing God to still you) when every fiber in your body wants to move and correct the situation.* Seer Meditation can be getting up in the morning, sitting in a chair and reflecting on God's works on a day when you have a million things to do and not a second to spare. It could be refraining from making a decision right away. It could be closing your eyes and taking three deep breaths before you transition from one place to the next. It could be the pause that you take before you respond to an unkind gesture or remark.

If obedience makes you open to God, then Seer Meditation allows you to stay open when your obedience seems pointless. We must give God some space for him to connect with us. There was a young girl who developed a very destructive habit of writing on anything she could reach. She would write on the walls, desks, floors, cabinets and even people. Her parents where extremely frustrated with her because she was ruining their home. The parents went to the girl's teacher for advice. They told the teacher the problem and then they began to recount all their failed attempts to remedy the problem. The teacher listened to all the parents said and responded, "Have you ever tried giving your daughter a board on which she could write? The problem is not that your daughter is writing. Writing at her age is a wonderful thing. The problem is that you have not given her an appropriate space to write in your home."

God is similar to this little girl. God constantly tries to communicate with us, to express his plans and visions for our lives. Yet often times we do not give God any space to write. We seldom set aside time for God to commune with us, so God attempts to get his message to us in the crux and corners of meetings, child pick-ups, dinner preparation, phone conversations, school days, work days and household chores. God writes on whatever he can get his hands on because the message he has for you is just that important. Reflect on one more subtle detail about the girl and her writing. When the girl writes on surfaces unintended for writing, the words that she scrolls are more difficult to see, but when she is given a board meant for writing, her words are seen clearly. The practice of Seer Meditation does not cause God to write, but it can provide God with a better surface to write on so we can read his message more clearly.

Seer Meditation not only provides space but it also provides us with a proper sense of time. There are so many instances when we are literally on the brink of a major breakthrough and we delay it or blow it all together because we could not be still and wait on the Lord. In most cases, there is a gap between obedience and its results. What so often ruins our blessings is what we do during that in-between time.

There was a young boy who wanted to do everything his father did. When he was old enough to go to the farm with his father he would say, "Dad, I want to be a farmer just like you." Each chance the boy had, he would go with his father and watch him plow the ground, plant seeds, water the fields and collect the harvest.

Eventually the boy asked the father for his own farm equipment and land. The father was amused by the boy's request. He found a small hoe, a water bucket and some seeds and gave it to his son. He sectioned off a part of the backyard and told the boy that it was his very own farmland. The father told the boy exactly what to do. He said, "Son, if you follow my instructions, I promise that you will have some vegetables growing on your farm." The boy was so excited. He plowed the ground until his arms were sore, then he scattered the seeds unto the ground and watered it. He went to his father and told him all that he did.

The next day, the boy got up early in the morning. He grabbed a bag and ran to collect his vegetables. When he came to his piece of land, he did not see any vegetables. He thought,

"Maybe the vegetables are underground and I have to dig them up." So he took his hoe and he began to dig into the ground looking for his vegetables, but he did not find any vegetables. When he looked around, he noticed he had dug up the seeds he had planted the previous day. He was devastated. He sat down and began to cry.

His father came over, thinking that the boy had hurt himself and said, "Son, what's wrong?" The son responded, "Dad, I did everything you said. I still didn't see any vegetables on my farmland." The father quietly responded, "Son, if you want to be a farmer, you must learn how to wait for the crop to grow."

So often we have done everything right. We have plowed. We have planted. We have watered. But when we do not see anything happening, we dig up our own garden. We never allow the seeds to take root. Being still and waiting on the Lord is not an easy task. What makes Seer Meditation so difficult is all the "stuff" that arises within us while we are trying to be still. Unwanted images, thoughts, and desires will arise during your meditation, but do not let them discourage you. Exterior stillness will lead to interior stillness and interior stillness allows us to be sensitive to the movement of God. Practice stillness while your blessings are taking root and emerging to the surface.

Conclusion

During Abram's deep sleep, he experienced a feeling of dread and received troubling news. Abram's desire to know what would occur prompted God to reveal possibly more than Abram wanted to know. God revealed part of the process that Abram's descendants would have to endure to secure the land.

God takes us through a process to prepare us to receive the blessings he has in store for us. If we saw all the processes that we will have to go through to walk into the bounty of God, then many of us would be more reluctant spiritual sojourners.

Be careful what you ask for; you just might get it. When you ask God for revelation, do not assume that all the insight he offers you is going to be glorious and beautiful. God will reveal some things to you about your family, your places of business, your friends, your community or yourself that might not be easy to receive.

Although most of us say we want to have greater clarity and confirmation, deep down inside we do not, and that is why we refuse to be still. We continue to go from place to place, focusing on work, focusing on family, talking on the phone, sitting in front of the computer screen, lying on the couch watching television, reading or preparing. We will do whatever it takes to prevent ourselves from finding an empty space and being still because of our fear of what we might discover in that stillness.

Abram also received the uplifting insight and confirmation that he desired. Once the fire descended upon the sacrifice, Abram received details about the land his descendants would possess. Fire often represented God's presence and guidance. Moses was called by God through "flames of fire"[9] in a bush. God led the Israelites into and through the wilderness with a "pillar of fire."[10] The book of Acts describes the Holy Spirit descending upon believers as "tongues of fire."[11] Elijah prepared a sacrifice, but allowed the "fire of the Lord"[12] to light the sacrifice to show that Yahweh was the one, true living God.

The torch of fire that descended upon Abram's sacrifice marked a transition in his relationship with Yahweh. Here,

Abram undoubtedly experienced the Lord's presence. There is no substitute for experience. Degrees and higher learning is great. The acquisition of new skills and knowledge always will have benefits, but nothing can replace on the job learning. That is where the greatest insight is gained. Abram obtained insight after he had experienced God.

Too many of us look for information about God, instead of experiencing God. Divine insight comes from your experience with God. God's insight is a gift. When this gift is unwrapped it exposes many blessings, as well as some burdens. Seer Meditation is a way to keep your arms open to receive the gift of God's insight. May you wisely use this gift.

Prayer

Everlasting God, we are so thankful that your grace is more enduring than our patience. May your assurance be felt during our planting season. Allow us to see that our labor is never in vain when we serve you. In the name of Jesus. Amen.

How to Sleep with God

Review
Goal: Become more open to God and aware of what God desires you to "see."
Premeditation: Worship.
Meditation: Stilling yourself and allowing God to still you.

Reflection
1) List three things that you waited a long time to receive. Did you ever receive them? How?

2) What did you learn about God in the process of waiting and receiving? What surprised you? What were confirmations?

3) What are some answers or insights you wish God would reveal to you now? Using Abram as your guide, what specific steps are you going to take to facilitate receiving those answers or insights?

Activity
Prepare a hot cup of water. Go to your prayer closet (or a place where you can quietly reflect and pray). Sit down and place the cup in front of you. Wait for the cup to become warm (almost cool). Meditate on the verse below, while you are waiting for the cup to cool. What God has for you is in the cup, but you cannot have it until it cools.

Meditation Verse
"Let there be light."[1]

Post-Meditation Questions
1) What was the most difficult aspect of being still?

2) What progress have you made in reference to patience?

3) What insights has God revealed to you through this meditation? How have these insights impacted your faith journey?

Chapter 3
Rocking Boat Meditation

Mark 4:35-41

We can learn a lot about a person by the way he or she handles adversity. We learn very little about political candidates when they are favored, are loved by everyone and have unlimited resources at their disposal. We see a glimpse of who they are when they come under public scrutiny, their approval rating starts to fall, and their resources become sparse. We have difficulty assessing a person's work performance during the holiday season when the office is lax and office parties abound. We get a sense of a person's ability when a deadline has been set and the demands are high. We do not notice an athlete's strength and stamina when they are in perfect health and having a picture-perfect night. We get a sense of an athlete's fortitude when the athlete has sustained an injury and the team needs him or her. We gain very little insight about building wealth from the person who started out with a million dollar trust fund. We gleam wisdom from the person who went from living on the streets to trading on Wall Street.

We learn little about people when everything is in place and all is running smoothly, but we learn the most about people when they do not have it all together and still move forward. If we gain insight about other people when they are in the midst of adversity, then what can God learn about us by the way we handle adversity?

The Goal

If we had to find a catchphrase for this passage in Mark, the phrase, "We are all in the same boat" would have to be considered. Jesus and the disciples were literally in the same boat. They were in the same boat that was rocking back and forth and flooded with water. They encountered the same storm. Yet the disciples were afraid and Jesus was at ease. The disciples were awake and Jesus was asleep. Jesus' abnormal response to the storm reveals the goal of Rocking Boat Meditation: to be at peace in chaotic situations.

The disciples were shocked at Jesus' reaction to the storm. They were surprised and bothered that Jesus was sleeping. Sometimes having a calm spirit during adversity will be more disturbing to others than showing panic. People expect you to show signs of distress when gas prices rise and job security is uncertain. They expect you will have an emotional breakdown when a close loved one has died. They anticipate you to be depressed when the doctor has given you a grim diagnosis. They look for you to fall apart when your relationship is in shambles.

Yet when your attitude and demeanor seem to contradict the situation you face, people often become even more uneasy and troubled. "Why don't you appear worried?" "Why aren't you freaking out?" "Why are you so calm and peaceful?" "What is the matter with you?" "You aren't upset?" You will be able to sleep through a storm, even when you are in the same rocking boat as everyone else, once competency in this meditation is achieved.

Premeditation

By the time we arrive at our passage in Mark, Jesus has already been baptized by John. The skies had already opened and God had shouted down, "This is my Son, whom I love; with him I am well pleased."[1] Jesus had already recruited his twelve disciples. He had already begun to cast out evil spirits, heal the lepers and empower the lame. He had already begun to preach, teach and correct the religious leaders. By this time in the gospel of Mark, Jesus had already begun doing what God had called him to do.

God's Will

The first action that you must take if you want to sleep through a storm is to become grounded in God's will for your life. Before you start complaining about how hectic your life is and how you feel frazzled all the time, ask yourself, "Am I using my life the way God would have me use it?" "Do I spend the majority of my time pursuing my will or God's will?" "Am I actively trying to figure out where God would have me to be, when God would have me to be there, and what God would have me to do once I get there?" The days when you get up early in the morning, run on the treadmill, fix breakfast, work all day on a tough project, come home, take the kids to their practices and rehearsals, pick up the kids, cook dinner for the family, wash the car and clean the house are the days when you sleep the best. If you want to have some divine peace, then you must start doing some God-centered work.

Imagine all that Jesus slept through. First, the windstorm began to rock the boat just a little, but Jesus kept on sleeping. The windstorm started rocking the boat more violently, but Jesus kept on sleeping. Waves started to crash up against the

51

boat, but Jesus kept on sleeping. The waves started to come into the boat, but Jesus kept on sleeping. The water flooded the boat, but Jesus kept on sleeping. Jesus did not wake up!

Some Christians can be at peace when the storm is out on the lake. Some Christians can remain at peace when their country is at war and they do not know anyone enlisted. They can be at peace when a distant relative dies. They can be at peace when kids they do not know have been getting into trouble. They can be at peace when unfamiliar organizations start cutting jobs. They can be at peace when people in the distance are getting ill. Some Christians can be at peace when the boat is rocking and waves are crashing outside the boat.

But can you be at peace when the water begins to flood your boat and you start to get wet? Can you be at peace when you personally know people stationed in war zones around the world? Can you be at peace when the people who raised you and were consistently present in your life are no longer there? Can you be at peace when it is your kids who are in trouble and causing headaches? Can you be at peace when your company starts to cut jobs? Can you be at peace when your friends and family get ill? Can you sleep when the waves start to crash into your boat and you become wet?

Jesus slept though all of that. Jesus prepared the stage for his meditative state by doing God's will before he set sail. We have biblical examples of people being out of line with God's will and not being able to sleep. King Xerxes could not sleep when he had forgotten to recognize Mordecai for the service Mordecai performed.[2] King Darius could not sleep when he allowed Daniel to be placed in a lion's den unjustly.[3] These men were not able to experience peace because they were so far from what God desired them to do. Rocking Boat Meditation is difficult to achieve when you are not fulfilling the tasks that God is leading you to perform.

There was a very popular teen band that sold millions of records across the world. Although the band was composed of five members, two members were clearly more talented than the rest. As the band grew older and the "teen" look began to fade, the manager proposed that the two most talented members form an adult duet. The first member thought the manager's idea was great. This member loved the money and fame that the teen group had brought him and did not want it to end. He figured this would be a perfect way to stay in the limelight. The second member also loved the money and the fame. He believed they could have a lot of success with the duet. Yet he felt the Lord was calling him to sing Christian music now.

The second member went to the first member and the manager and proposed that they create a Christian duet. Since all of them were Christians, he thought it would be a great idea. Both the first member and the manager objected to the suggestion. They said that singing Christian music is the same amount of work for less money, which did not make sense. So, the two band members parted ways. The first member went on to have a successful secular singing career and the second one went on to have a successful career as a Christian artist.

Years pass and the two former band members coincidentally meet on a plane. They are seated next to one another. They catch up on all that has happened over the years and they reminisce about the good old days. Midway into the flight, the plane begins to experience some heavy turbulence. The plane is caught in a severe thunderstorm and cannot fly above it. The storm is so intense and causes the plane to shake so much that the oxygen masks become available to the passengers. Children begin to cry. Some people begin to pray and others experience panic attacks. The pilot makes a few references to an emergency landing.

In the midst of all this turmoil, the Christian musician puts his head back, closes his eyes and begins humming a soft tune. The other artist turns to him and says, "How can you be so calm? We might have to land suddenly. We could be injured or even die." Without even opening his eyes, the Christian artist responds, "I am calm because if I die today I am confident that I did what God wanted me to do."

The Christian artist would have never experienced the peace he had on the plane if he had not heeded God's voice and surrendered his career to God. His obedience to God's will preceded his peace. Your peace is strongly connected to what you do before you need comfort and stability. The successful practice of Rocking Boat Meditation is connected to how faithful you are to God before you begin the meditation.

Meditation

Jesus slept while the disciples reflected on their turmoil and possible demise. His sleep contrasted the disciples' reflections of worry and panic. Jesus went to the stern or hind part of the boat to sleep. The stern was the place where the anchors were kept. Jesus was in the place that held the objects that could stabilize the boat in a storm. This was a fitting place for Jesus, because he had a special way of grounding the chaotic situations of life in fundamental truths about God's law and God's nature. When everyone was ready to stone a woman for her sins, he grounded the situation in God's forgiveness and mercy.[4] When a woman shouted and chased down Jesus to ask for a miracle, Jesus grounded the situation in the power of faith.[5] When the guards came to arrest Jesus and one of his disciples sought to defend him with a weapon, Jesus grounded the situation in God's everlasting protection.[6]

In each chaotic situation you encounter, you must drop some anchors. Facing the inevitability of death can be a frightening situation. But when you drop the anchor of eternal life in the midst of dying, you are stabilized. A nasty breakup can be a devastating experience. But when you drop the anchor of God's steadfast love in the midst of heartache, you are stabilized. Financial troubles can be emotionally draining. But when you drop the anchor of God's heavenly treasure, you are stabilized. Dreams deferred can be disappointing. But when you drop the anchor of God's divine assurances, you are stabilized. *Rocking Boat Meditation is when you reflect on and pronounce the promises of God in the midst of your storms.* Notice I did not say the storm would go away, but you can have security in the midst of the storm.

Considerations

Jesus imposed his divine peace on an external situation. As you mature in your relationship with Christ, not only will you be at peace in chaotic situations, but you can also be a vehicle to help make chaotic situations peaceful. You want to get to a point in your Christian walk where the divine peace that you carry around influences, affects and alters the environments that you occupy.

One of the crucial elements to being able to quiet turbulent circumstances is your ability to properly classify a situation. Let us examine the nature of a windstorm. The Spirit of God was often associated with the wind. In other words, the disciples were not simply encountering some turbulent times. They were experiencing turbulent times that involved a spiritual component.

The disciples' apparent concern was over the water that was being pushed into the boat; however, the true cause of their problem was not the water but the wind. The wind was the force behind the water. Most storms that you encounter in your life have some wind. Most of the troubling times that you go through have a spiritual component. You must learn to identify and then address the spiritual components (both positive and negative) of any situations that you encounter.

Jesus' words were more than just a pronouncement for new weather, but a counter to a spiritual attack. In each Synoptic gospel (Matthew, Mark and Luke) the account of Jesus calming the storm is followed by Jesus' encounter with a demoniac at Gerasenes. The storm could have been a demonic attack to prevent the liberation that would occur at the shore where Jesus' boat was to land. We must understand the condition of the demon possessed man[7] in all three gospels to appreciate the magnitude of his liberation and why his liberation would be resisted so fiercely by the demonic world.

Unclean Spirit

The first description that the Gospels give to this man is that he is controlled by demons. These demons are later described in many translations as an unclean spirit. An unclean object was considered unfit for God's people and out of line with God's intended order. I believe the modern day reader has greater difficulty brushing off the reality of demons when they are placed in the context of unfitness for God.

As a pastor, I am witnessing a growing trend in the Church to disregard the notions of demons and even hell. Many Christians are open to consider that the Gospel writers mean many things when they speak of demons as long as they do not have to entertain the possibility that demons actually mean demons. Our characters of demons in popular culture have crippled our spiritual sensibilities. We miss the point when we debate what demons look like or what form they present themselves. Our focus should be that the Gospel writers identified forces, thoughts and intentions unfit for God's intended order that had power in the world and consumed peoples' lives. This man was possessed by something that was unclean and needed to be cleansed by God's grace through Jesus Christ.

If I ask a group of Christians have they ever been possessed by a demon or demons, most would answer no. Yet if I asked the same people have they ever been controlled by some addictions, habits, commitments, mentalities or priorities that are not fit for a disciple of Christ and out of line with God's will, then most of their answers would change. This man's possession is no different from our possessions. This man's need for deliverance was no greater than our need.

No Clothes

The second aspect of this man's condition is that he had no clothes. Throughout the biblical culture, clothing reflected one's emotional and spiritual state. For example, during times of feasting and celebration, people wore their finest robes. This clothing reflected their joyous state, but also their understanding that they were recipients of God's blessings. During times of mourning or fasting, people wore sackcloth, a harsh, unattractive covering. This clothing reflected a somber state, but also reflected one's understanding that they had sinned against God and desired God's mercy. Clothing in many instances indicated an acknowledgement and pursuit of God's grace either in good times or bad times.

This man wore no fine robes, plain garments or sackcloth, but wore no garments at all. He was naked. If clothes partly represented one's relationship to God and acknowledgement of God, his lack of clothes indicated in some ways an unawareness of his need for God's grace.

Tombs

The last aspect that we must understand about this man's condition was his residence. He lived among the tombs. This man had surrounded himself with death.

Romans 6:23 states, "For the wages of sin is death." Likewise, Proverbs 14:12 reads, "There is a way that seems right to a man, but in the end it leads to death." When we begin to operate outside the order and will of God, we are literally flirting with dead things. We are setting up our homes in the graveyards similar to this man.

This man's condition left him out of line with God's order, unaware of his need for God's grace and surrounded by death. He was in the most devastating of spiritual chokeholds and Jesus was headed in his direction.

Many times the intensity of the storm we experience is directly correlated to the magnitude of the glory that God is about to receive. The storm raged against the boat not because Jesus and the disciples were in the water, but because of where they were headed and who they were about to meet. Ephesians 6:12 tells us, "For our struggle is not against flesh and blood, but against the rulers, against the authorities, against the powers of this dark world and against spiritual forces of evil in the heavenly realms."[8] The writer of Ephesians tells us clearly stop focusing on the waves, the water, the boat and the rocking, and start focusing on the spiritual forces at work. Address the spiritual concerns (forces, thoughts, intentions and energy not of God) before attempting to improve any situation.

Conclusion

I often joke if only people were as faithful as demons. There is a lot we can learn from a demon, even in the midst of spiritual attack. The demons at Gerasenes performed some acts, to which Christians should aspire. First, the demons acknowledged the presence of Christ. As soon as Jesus came on shore, the demons went to him. Mark even notes that they worshiped him.[9] How many Christians go days, weeks or months without praying, attending church or acknowledging God in anyway?

Second, the demons at Gerasenes were united in their domination of this man. They understood that their stronghold over the man would be greater if more of them possessed him. If more Christians, churches and pastors could embrace the notion of unity over competition and jealously, God's kingdom would have a greater presence in our world. If we came together as a "legion" to possess this world, how strong would our presence be?

Lastly, the demons displayed stubbornness and persistence. Once Jesus commanded the demons to come out of the man, they began to negotiate with Jesus. They began to ask questions. They showed some resistance. What if Christians were as determined to possess the world as these demons were committed to possess this man? We too easily forfeit the dreams and aspirations that God has for us out of convenience, laziness or fatigue.

Rocking Boat Meditation shows you how to sleep through a storm. This sleep is not an escape from our problems, but conscious resistance. It is awareness of the true nature of the storm. Because we are aware of the storm's origin and purpose, we find peace in the storm and joy in the liberation that is coming on the shore. When it is your time to sleep, do not allow any person, event or occasion to wake you up.

Prayer

All powerful Master, there is no thunder that you cannot silence. There is no wind that you cannot still. There is no storm that you cannot calm. When we are shaken and frightened by the circumstances of life, may we rest assured in your love for us. Amen.

How to Sleep with God

Review
Goal: A peaceful state in the midst of chaos.
Premeditation: Ground yourself in God's will for your life.
Meditation: To reflect and pronounce the promises of God in the midst of chaotic circumstances.

Reflection
1) List three of the most difficult times in your life. What kept you stable then?

2) List three areas of your life now where you need greater stability and peace.

3) What steps can you take to move from the position of the frantic disciples to the peaceful master when you enter a storm?

Activity

Write a promise of God on a small piece of paper. Use Bible verses to support your beliefs. Carry the paper around with you during the day. Throughout the day, pull out the paper and pronounce it to yourself between deep breaths. You may substitute the meditation verse for a promise when you desire.

Meditation Verse

Peace, be still.[1]

Post-Meditation Questions

1) Why did you pick the promise that you did?

2) How can you extend God's promise to others?

3) How did you feel when you pronounced your promise?

Chapter 4
Conscious Meditation

2nd Samuel 11:1-12

Conscientious Objector is a name you do not hear often.
Those born in the last few decades might not even know what
the term means. For generations to lose memory of this term is
more than a loss of history, but also has spiritual significance.
To forget individuals whose beliefs moved them to object to
war (at the risk of alienation, imprisonment and chastisement)
is to forget a powerful example of how the world of the unseen
guides us. I wonder, has our current environment lost the
power of the exercise of conscious? There are many ways that
people act based on their conscious, yet it is often at little cost
or even greater reward to them. Many people refrain from
eating meat based on their conscious, but then consume veggie
chicken or beef products. They exercise their conscious and still
enjoy the flavor and taste of meat. Some refrain from wearing
furs, conflict diamonds or clothes made in sweatshops. These
same people many times turn their acts of resistance or
restraint into badges of honor. They take so much pride in
them that they use them as weapons against anyone that does
not conform to their standards. Objections, resistance, and
restraint based on one's conscious seem more palatable and
convenient today. How can we exercise our conscious in an
authentic way? This is a question that we must pose and
attempt to answer continuously and vigorously.

The Goal

The book of Samuel gives us a prime example of a person that exercises his conscious. Uriah was a soldier in the Israelite army. King David offered him an opportunity that every soldier dreamed about: permission to see his wife and enjoy the comforts of his home for an evening. Uriah refused to experience these benefits out of concern for his fellow soldiers. This act sets the goal for Conscious Meditation, which is to cultivate reflections that sustain sensitivity and awareness to the plight of others.

Premeditation

There are a couple of conditions that allowed Uriah to meditate on the circumstances of the soldiers. Uriah's meditation was directly tied to his experience. He reflected on the plight of the soldiers because he had just left them. Contact with a particular group, environment or circumstances creates a context for Conscious Meditation.

When I expressed my desire to become a seminary professor to my mentor, he advised me to serve in the church before I taught in seminary. He said, "You can always tell which professors have served in the church from those that have not." When I attended seminary, I understood exactly what he meant. Professors voided of any experience in the church seemed to be cut off from certain considerations. Their style and delivery of theological concepts or biblical information lacked a certain grain of sensitivity, which topics so dear to people's hearts required. At worst, these professors were intentionally confrontational and condescending about the certainty of their positions and the impossibility of other options. They had turned their theories into gods and blindly followed them where ever they led. Many of these professors embodied the characteristics that they attempted to teach against: rigidness, lack of creativity, and close mindedness.

The reflections and sensitivities that these professors lack are normally gained while serving in the church. When you minister to a mother who lost her teenage son, your theological language softens. When you serve communion to someone in a hospital bed or a death bed, your understanding of the Lord's Supper is impacted. When you marry a couple and then lead them through counseling five years later, your conception of the Greek or Hebrew definitions of love are forever altered. When you baptize a fifty year old woman, who accepted Christ in her life for the first time, your view of conversion is forever changed. Certain reflections, considerations and sensitivities are birthed by contact with people, circumstances and environments.

Some of the most influential and famous theologians also ministered to people or serve churches some time in their lives. St. Augustine was a pastor and bishop. Karl Barth served as a pastor of a small country church. Martin Luther King Jr. was a pastor and Civil Rights Leader. Howard Thurman served as a pastor and chaplain. The list could continue. What would their theologies be without their experience in the church? What would their ideas be without their experience in service to others? What made their ideas, theories, and insights so lofty and powerful was that they contain reflections, considerations, and sensitivities birthed in the humility of service and contact with the mystical body of Christ called the church.

Similar to Uriah, our Conscious Meditation begins to emerge with an experience or encounter. Uriah not only experienced battle and the living circumstances of the soldiers,

65

but he also discussed them with King David. As soon as Uriah went to the palace David asked him to give a report of all that was occurring. Uriah recounted and remembered the circumstances he left. This discussion also set the context for his meditation.

Some people experience a circumstance or event and then try as hard as they can to suppress it. They do not want to talk or think about it. Of course, this does not erase the memory of the experience, but just pushes it beyond the conscious level. This push makes it difficult for Conscious Meditation to occur. Uriah's experience and discussion with the king set the stage for his meditation.

Meditation

Uriah had been pulled from the battlefield and whisked off to David's palace where he was asked to talk about what he had just left. His fellow soldiers and the place he recently departed were on his mind. He could not help but to reflect upon them. In this context, Uriah slept. He slept as he meditated on the people, place and circumstances he left. Two important descriptions about Uriah's sleep inform the nature of Conscious Meditation.

Refuses to Go Home

Uriah did not go home. He refused to enjoy the benefits of his trip. He denied himself the comfort to share a bed with his wife, refresh himself and relax in his home. The consideration of his soldiers and previous environment caused him to reflect upon a way to deny himself.

Conscious Meditation involves reflection on how you can live with less as a result of particular people, circumstances or environments, which you have experienced. For example, with this meditation, you might reflect upon how to refrain from certain electronic conveniences for a day once you have stayed in a country where electricity is a luxury not a God-given right. You might reflect on your over dependence or indulgence with the Internet after you visit places where people travel distances just to check their email. You might reflect upon how you could eat less when you encounter families that cannot afford three meals a day. You might reflect upon how to make more sacrifices at your job when you encounter family or friends who have loss employment. *Conscious Meditation leads us to consider how we can deny ourselves as way to maintain our awareness of the plight of others.*

A call even to reflect upon consuming, having, and doing less, seems counter-intuitive in our society. Moderation could be considered a lost art. Why would anyone want to be moderate, when she or he can have it all is what our commercials and advertisements tells us. Yet, ironically, having it all is a most unfulfilling, unsatisfactory feeling. Having it all always leads to the constant pursuit of having more. The belief that there is always more to obtain never allows rest, but always to pursue, and therefore to never be satisfied. Conscious Meditation causes us to slow down and think about how we can live a more moderate life in honor of the lives of others.

In the Entrance

Once Uriah refused to sleep at his home, he decided to lay his head at the palace entrance. Uriah's sleep accommodations mirrored the sleep arrangements of the soldiers he left. His fellow soldiers were in makeshift homes. Where Uriah chose to stay also represented transience. The entrance to the palace positioned him between two worlds: a world of royalty and commoners, rulers and followers, the haves and the have-nots. Uriah, in a symbolic sense, slept in between these two worlds, not having a place of his own.

Uriah's act precedes the witness and words of Jesus. Many people are uncomfortable with regarding Jesus as a homeless person. But how are we to take Jesus' words in the Gospel of Matthew? When a scribe came to Jesus and proclaimed to follow Jesus wherever he went, Jesus responded, "Foxes have holes and birds of the air have nests, but the Son of Man has nowhere to lay His head."[2] At the very least, Jesus' words imply that following him would require a transient lifestyle. His twelve closest disciples certainly lived such a lifestyle. They traveled to different houses and towns, preaching the gospel and healing the sick. They relied on the kindness of the people they encountered for food, clothing, and shelter. They sacrificed material security and stability to follow Christ. They were on the move, not residing in one particular place during their years of ministry.

Jesus and his disciples not only mirrored Uriah in transience, but also in being in between two worlds. Jesus was a precarious figure who could not be associated with one particular group. Pastors, theologians, and those fighting for social justice often point out that Jesus associated with the outcasts of society. He reached out to the lepers and prostitutes. He ministered to the blind beggars. He was a man of the people. Yet Jesus also associated with the wealthy and privileged of society. He befriended many tax collectors, those who were wealthy by dishonest gain, and even took one as his disciple. He ate at the house of Pharisees and members of the

Sanhedrin. He enjoyed the comfort of Mary and Martha's home on many occasions. Jesus was a person who constantly crossed boundaries and interacted with different people. He did not interact with one group, but was in between and among many groups at different times. Jesus' life embodied Uriah's singular gesture of sleeping in the palace entrance.

Conscious Meditation involves reflection upon how to connect with others outside our comfort zone. This meditation leads us to ask ourselves questions such as, "What groups of people don't I interact with and why?" "What people or groups am I limited to and why?" "Around who do I feel most comfortable and least comfortable, and why?" A life void of tension is a life void of growth. Sometimes the necessary tension that we lack comes from interacting with people who have different worldviews, thoughts and experiences than our own. Jesus placed himself in the midst of the tension between rich and poor, Jew and Gentile, master and servant, healthy and sick. This same tension assists us to have a greater connection to and understanding of our community and world.

David Reflects Lack of Conscious

Uriah's refusal to go home and his choice to sleep at the palace entrance revealed a strong connection to the soldiers he left. His awareness and sensitivity to others provides an excellent model for Conscious Meditation. If Uriah exemplifies someone with a conscious, then King David embodies a man in need of one. Because of David's willful disconnection from the army, he lacked the sensitivity and awareness needed to be conscious.

David's disconnection produced a lack of sensitivity and his lack of sensitivity morphed into full fledged disregard for

Sleeping with God

another's marriage. While David was disengaged from war and the soldiers that were fighting for him, he saw a beautiful woman bathing. He summoned his servants to retrieve her, they had intercourse, and eventually David discovered that she was pregnant. This pregnant woman's husband was Uriah and hence begins David's elaborate plan to cover up his adultery.

David's adultery with Uriah's wife and his eventual murder of Uriah all begin with a simple decision not to fight with his army. The winter was a time when battle was suspended. Kings rested during this season and when spring came, they resumed fighting. The new season of spring was an indication that a transition from resting mode to battle mode must be made. But David never made the transition. He did not respond to the demands of his position or the season. David decided not to go to war with his army and became disconnected from his soldiers in distance and experience. While David resided in the palace, his soldiers resided on the battle field. While David experienced the luxury and comforts of royalty, his soldiers lived in the harsh and inconvenient conditions of war.

As king, David did not perform the activities that allowed him to obtain the throne, namely fighting with the people in the name of the Lord. One of David's greatest attributes was that he was a fearless and skilled warrior. He was a man of the people. He came from humble beginnings. He was the youngest in his family. He could relate to the commoner and the underdog. One of David's greatest attributes was that he was connected to the people. That connection was severely impaired when David decided to stay in the palace while all the others went to fight.

Often times, the goal in our society is to be disconnected. Many people aspire to live in a gated community, separated from the communities not in the same socio-economic background. Some aspire to be the boss so they can be distinct from all the employees. Some aspire to be the leader so they can be detached from the masses. Some aspire to acquire certain possessions so they can display their higher status. All separation has consequences. Separation can be extremely destructive when it breeds insensitivity and lack of regard for others. David allowed his separation to lead him down a destructive path.

Conscious Meditation is one way to safeguard us against the desensitizing nature of society and the illusion of being the exception. Uriah and David provide two very different examples of how to live in society. David chose to disconnect from others, focus on self-gratification and disregard the plight of others. Uriah chose to stay connected, practiced self-denial and remember the plight of others. Only by choosing the path of Uriah will our world be a sustainable place to live.

Prayer

God of all creation, remind us that you are the God of other nations, other people, other communities and even the God of our enemies. May we see that no woman or man is an island, but connected to your people. Expose our insensitivities and ignorance so that we can better display your love. Amen.

How to Sleep with God

Review
Goal: to cultivate reflections that foster sensitivity and awareness of the plight of others.
Premeditation: Experience of others' circumstances.
Meditation: Consider methods of self-denial that keep you sensitive to others and consider how to connect with others outside your comfort zone.

Reflection Questions
1) Can you identify a time in your life when you were like David, unaware and insensitive to a particular community's circumstances? Explain.

2) What caused your awareness to change or remain the same concerning that particular community?

3) How can you become more like Uriah in your everyday life—sensitive to the plight of others?

4) Where do you think Conscious Meditation is most needed in our society? Why?

5) Give a modern day example of a person who embodies Conscious Meditation.

Activity
Find a newspaper or magazine that cover international news. Pick one article about a community in another part of the world. Reflect upon how you are connected to that community. Meditate on how you are tied to the individuals in that community from various perspectives (i.e., economic, social, biological, ecological, historical, etc.).

Meditation Verse
Body of Christ

Post Reflection Questions
1) Which community did you pick? Why?

2) How challenging was the meditation for you? Explain why?

3) Did your reflection lead you to any new insights?

Chapter 5
Walking Dead Reverse Meditation

Mark 5:21-24, 35-43

What is more controversial, more politicized and maybe even more glamorized about the criminal justice system than the last-minute stay of execution? The prisoner eats his last meal and is taken from the cell. As he walks those last steps to the execution room, the whole prison acknowledges that he is as good as dead, hence the term dead man walking. Though the prisoner is still breathing and walking, he is regarded as already gone to everyone who views him. He is strapped into the chair. A priest says some prayers. As the execution is ready to take place, the phone rings and orders are given to stay the execution. New DNA evidence surfaces. A pending Supreme Court case needs to be considered. The mental capacity of the prisoner is questioned. The fairness of the trial is challenged. Whatever the reason or cause, the prisoner everyone regards as dead is given another opportunity to live.

The Goal

The account of Jairus' daughter holds many similarities to a last-minute stay of execution. She had people fighting for her life. Once a certain amount of time transpired, many people thought that no hope was left and she was dead. The crowd could only see a dead person, but Jesus was able to intervene and pull the girl out of the execution chair. In his act of pulling this girl "off of death row," we discover the intent of Walking Dead Reverse Meditation. The goal of this reverse meditation is to enlighten the consciousness of those regarded as hopelessly lost or those parts of us that we regard as beyond all hope. After practicing this form of reverse meditation, one should be awakened from pessimistic meditative states.

Jairus realized that his daughter had reached a dire state. He felt that the situation was deteriorating quickly and only Jesus could help her. Yet the assistance that Jarius petitioned from Jesus is much more than a request for his daughter not to be sick. This account in the gospel of Mark uses two words that cannot be hastily overlooked: *sozo*, which the King James Version and New International Version translate as to heal, and *zoe*, which is rendered in the two translations as to live. First, let's deal with *sozo*.

Sozo — Healed & Saved

One cannot possess an accurate view of the society of Jesus without grasping the spiritual and religious understanding of being clean. Jesus was born into a culture in which being unclean or clean revealed one's relationship to God. To be clean indicated one was aligned with God, while to be unclean showed one was misaligned with God. Being clean or unclean was a physical manifestation of an inner spiritual state. A person who had an undesirable physical state, such as leprosy, blindness or paralysis, was regarded as being misaligned with God. The person's perverse spiritual state revealed itself in his or her physical illness. If one was physically healed, then one would go to the temple to be examined by the priest, perform the prescribed rituals and afterwards could be restored as clean.

One of Jesus' major clashes with the religious establishment was over how these terms of clean and unclean should be applied to individuals. Jesus transcended this context. As opposed to the religious establishment, Jesus held that one's physical condition had no correlation to one's inner spiritual state. Jesus believed that one could be healed even if one's body was not physically cured, hence the word *sozo* can be translated as both to save and to heal.

For Jesus, healing was a spiritual occurrence first that could have physical implications. At times, Jesus separated the physical cure from the inward restoration maybe to make this crucial theological statement. The woman who interrupts Jesus on his way to Jairus' house is a classic example of the uniqueness of Jesus' healing power.[1]

The unnamed woman, known only by her condition of uncontrollable bleeding, saw Jesus in a crowd. She made her way through the crowd. Then she reached out to touch Jesus' garment. The woman believed that even the slightest physical contact with Jesus could alleviate her condition. After contact with Jesus was made, the woman's disease vanished, but the woman experienced a different type of restoration once she returned to Jesus. The Gospel of Mark reads, "But the woman fearing and trembling, knowing what was done in her, came and fell down before him, and told him all the truth. And he said unto her, Daughter, thy faith hath made thee whole; go in peace, and be whole of thy plague."[2] If the woman only needed her bleeding to stop, then why did she return to Jesus? If the woman was complete after her condition vanished, then why did Jesus command her to be whole? Although this woman's condition was cured, her soul was not at peace. She touched Jesus physically to be cured, but Jesus needed to touch her spiritually to be redeemed.

The distinction between this woman's cure and her healing is also reflected in Mark's choice of words. When Mark refers to the woman's physical restoration in verse 29, he uses the Greek word *iaomoi*. When the gospel writer refers to the woman's state after Jesus sends her off in peace, he uses the Greek word *sozo*. I am certainly not suggesting that every word variation (found in Mark or the Scriptures in general) implies a radical shift in meaning, however the word choice is worthy of note.

The paralytic who is lowered down from a roof to receive a miracle from Jesus displays another clear example of Jesus' form of healing.[3] A man who was paralyzed heard that Jesus arrived in town. His friends took him to the house where Jesus ministered to the people, but the house was so full they could not enter. So the paralytic's friends lowered the man down into the house from the roof. Jesus acknowledged their faith and forgave the paralytic of his sins. With the bleeding woman, Jesus cured her first then healed her, but with the paralytic Jesus healed the man first, then cured him. This man's reconciliation with God was a much greater miracle than to fix his inability to walk. Jesus asked the skeptics in the crowd, "Which is easier, to say to the paralytic, 'Your sins are forgiven you,' or to say, 'Arise, take up your bed and walk?'"[4] In this question, Jesus challenges the scribes' and our notions of what a miracle is and more specifically, what it means to be healed. The moment this man was forgiven, he was healed. I believe Jesus separates the act of forgiveness from the physical restoration to show that one does not equal the other (although they can come together).

When Jairus asked Jesus to heal (*sozo*) his daughter, he was not simply saying to make her healthy again. He was asking Jesus to save her, get her aligned with God. Whether Jairus had a view of healing that was more reflective of the religious establishment or a view that reflected Jesus' new spiritual consciousness, the implications of Jairus' request involved spiritual restoration as well as a physical healing.

Zoe—Life

Similarly, the term *zoe* has deeper implications. When Jairus petitions for Jesus to allow his daughter to "live," we often perceive this request as simply a request for continued physical existence. Yet we all know people who are physically alive, but emotionally or spiritually dead. We all know people who are physically alive, but have no hope and are dead. Living is not simply the pumping of the heart and the circulation of blood through our bodies; living involves a meaningful way of being. It involves having a purpose. Hence Christ states, "I am the bread of life"[5] and "I am the resurrection and the life."[6] In Christ "was life, and that life was the light of men."[7] Jairus was asking that his daughter have a richer, fuller life than she had before. Jesus was asked to provide this girl not simply with a longer life, but also a distinctively different and better life.

Negative Meditation

In these two key terms—*sozo* and *zoe*—we uncover the profundity of Jairus' request and receive a sketch of the girl's meditative state. Jesus mentions sleep after her negative meditative state is implied. If Jairus requested that his daughter be aligned with God, then he was also suggesting that she was participating in activities that led her astray. If Jairus requested that his daughter have a richer, fuller life, then he was also suggesting that she was not living up to her God-given potential.

The daughter's state parallels many of the negative meditative states found in our modern society. Think about all the activities that our young people are engaged in today that lead them from the church. Think about the proliferation of gangs and teenage promiscuity. Think about the variety of video games, television dramas and movies. Think about our society's obsession and glamorization with becoming an athlete, actor, model or singer. Ponder all this and then ask yourself, "Is my child being lured into a destructive meditative state?" "Is my nephew, niece, youth group, neighbor being lured into a destructive meditative state?" "Am I being lured into a destructive meditative state?" Often our context is structured to lure us to sleep.

Reverse Meditation

As Jesus walked to Jairus' home, someone informed Jairus and the crowd with Jesus that the girl was dead. Jesus disregarded those words and continued to the house. Once he arrived at the house, he notified the mourners that the girl was not dead but asleep.

Jesus took a few significant actions to bring this girl out of her sleep. First, Jesus properly diagnosed the girl's condition. Jesus told the people in the household that the girl's state was not permanent.

I knew a woman who began to experience severe abdominal pain. She went to her doctor and had a number of tests performed. The doctor concluded that the only way the pain would subside was if she had major surgery. She became very disturbed by the news and feared undergoing surgery. After a week of worrying and dealing with the pain, she felt like she had no choice. She would schedule the surgery. Right before she picked up the phone to call her doctor, her husband suggested that she get a second opinion. He told her, "What could be the harm?"

She went to see another doctor and he examined her. He told her if she changed her diet, her pain would subside in less than a month. The woman had one condition, but two radically different diagnoses. Jesus was Jairus' second opinion. Jesus brought a diagnosis into the home that was not as dire and pessimistic as the first one that everyone had accepted. He identified that the situation had more hope and possibility than the household believed.

Framing a situation appropriately is a vital part of Walking Dead Reverse Meditation. Christ has given you too much to be seduced by the pessimism of the natural world. This does not mean that you create a fantasy world for yourself, where you believe death, destruction or an end will never occur. Framing a situation appropriately means that as a person of faith you will not have the same diagnosis as a non-believer although you are both seeing the same condition.

Once Jesus offered his second opinion, everyone in the house laughed at him, and Jesus responded by putting them out of the house. Why did Jesus respond this way? Did he do it out of anger? Did he do it because they embarrassed him or challenged him? A pattern emerges in our passage of Mark with Jesus and people of disbelief: Jesus separates from them.

A crowd followed Jesus to Jairus' home. Before they arrived at the home, someone reported that the girl was dead and therefore it was pointless for Jesus to go to the home. After this report came, Jesus separated from the crowd and allowed only Peter, James and John to come with him. Jesus separated from the crowd in the house after he heard the laughter at his diagnosis. Jesus refused to have anyone near him who believed all hope was gone. Jesus understood that the girl would not benefit from two competing diagnoses.

Jesus had a clear sense of the destructive nature of doubt. He had encountered person after person, who were perfectly positioned to receive God's blessing, but became sidetracked by doubt. Jesus encountered a group of people looking to be fed.[8] They requested that Jesus miraculously provide bread for them, so their doubts about him could be settled. While they asked for bread to alleviate their doubts, they missed the fact that Jesus was the bread of life. When Jesus returned to his hometown to preach and heal, the people's doubts prevented their renewal. The Gospel of Mark reads, "Now He could do no mighty work there, except that He laid His hands on a few sick people and healed them. And He marveled because of their unbelief. Then He went about the villages in a circuit, teaching."[9] The people's doubt blocked a magnificent demonstration from God. Jesus encountered a thief on a cross whose doubt caused him to lose a seat in paradise.[10] These are a few examples among the many times where Jesus watched people squander God's grace.

Free will is a double edge sword. With it we can experience the wisdom and glory of God. But with it we can also do ourselves tremendous harm and miss so much of what God offers. Doubt is a much more powerful element than most realized. Jesus understood its power and influence on situations and separated from those who held it.

There comes a point in every situation, every relationship, and every predicament when you have to make a decision about what course of action you will take. To surround yourself with reasons why you will fail is to engage in self-sabotage. Some situations are too important to have doubters coming along for the ride. *Walking Dead Reverse Meditation involves the minimization of doubt and the maximization of hope.* Ceasing to reflect on doubt and shifting to reflections of hope is key.

Jesus took the girl's hand and commanded her to arise. Throughout the Gospel accounts, physical contact is a vital component of many of Jesus' healings. When Jesus descended down a mountain, a man with leprosy ran to him and asked to be healed. Jesus touched the man and commanded him to be healed.[11] Jesus entered the house of Peter's mother-in-law and recognized she was sick, so "he touched her hand and the fever left her."[12] This power of touch is also extended to the disciples. The resurrected Christ tells his disciples some of the signs that a believer will display. One of these is that "they will place their hands on sick people, and they will get well."[13] Certainly, Jesus did not touch all people whom he healed, but physical contact seemed to be a pivotal part of many of his healings.

An elder of mine told me about his initial response to the emerging political and social climate of sexual harassment awareness. He began refraining from touching and hugging anyone—especially someone of the opposite sex—because he feared the gesture could be misconstrued. A simple gesture could be defined as harassment. Any type of touch could be grounds for a lawsuit. Yet after taking this stance for a while, he came to another conclusion: "People need to be touched." There is something about the power of a touch that transcends even the most eloquently constructed and inspiring sermon.

After my first semester of divinity school, some of my classmates gathered and compared their impressions of our ministry training ground. One classmate, who had not visited her home all semester, said, "I don't think I have felt someone touch me this entire semester. I miss that." Once our conversation was over, I placed my hand on her shoulder (but was still a bit reluctant to give her a hug). Physical contact is an extremely vital part of human existence.

Yes, Jesus had the ability to heal by his very words or thoughts. Yet there were a few people's situations that yearned for not just a healing, but for physical contact. There were some people that needed the power that only a touch could deliver. Jesus touched Jairus' daughter because he realized that her situation called for his physical involvement.

There are some people you can assist with sound words of advice, or proper instruction, or a check. Other people's situations require that you get your hands dirty; they require your direct involvement, your physical touch. Jesus touched the little girl because her situation called for the physicality of God.

The love of God is shown to us by Jesus' death on the cross, but it is also displayed to us through the Incarnation. God took on the physicality of humanity because he loved us. God was embodied in a clay vessel, which could experience pain, aging, disappointment, sadness and betrayal, all because God wanted to be closer to us. Only an extremely naïve person could think that a situation is in drastic need of improvement, but feel exempt from making physical contact with it. *Walking Dead Reverse Meditation calls for your physical involvement in a situation.* It calls for your time, energy and sometimes your undivided attention.

Lastly, Walking Dead Reverse Meditation involves perpetual concern. You must have an interest in the well-being of a person or situation after all appears to be on the right track.

Before Jesus left the home of the girl, he commanded her family to give her something to eat. Jesus was concerned about the girl after she was healed. He wanted to make sure she had everything she needed, even after he left.

So often we like to view healing as an event, but healing is more similar to a process. The girl was alive, but there was still some follow-up that needed to be done. No matter how much help you offer or work you perform, you cannot simply walk away after progress is seen. Maybe this will involve some check-ins, referrals or getting needed resources. Continual reflection on the situation is essential for this form of reverse meditation.

Conclusion

We have a lot of dead men and women walking. We have many people who have been crushed by tragedy, paralyzed by physical and mental poverty or hypnotized by materialism and violence. Each time we see them, we shake our heads in pity or roll our eyes in disgust. Let me tell you a secret. *They are not dead, they are only sleeping.* Yes, you can laugh if you wish, when you hear someone say that it is possible for trances of depression to be broken. You can laugh when you hear that poverty can be eliminated. Yes, you can laugh when you hear someone say that words such as weapons and guns will become unfamiliar terms to future generations. Yes, you can laugh when you hear that internal forms of beauty will be the standards for judging others. Yes, you can laugh when someone says, "They are not dead, but they are only sleeping." But, at the end of the day, you must make a choice. Do you want to be the one who is put out of the house for laughing or do you want to be the one to help wake up these dormant parts of society? The choice is yours.

Prayer

God of new life, resurrect our sleeping hopes and visions. Where there is death, expose your possibility. Where there is loss and fear, inspire us to rise above them. May our laughter at a transformed world cease, so we may contribute to your kingdom on earth. Amen.

How to Awake with God

Review
Goal: Enlighten hopelessly lost parts of ourselves, family and society.

Negative Meditation: Engagement in activities and mindsets devoid of God.

Reverse Meditation:
• Framing
• Minimization of doubt and maximization of hope
• Physical involvement
• Perpetual concern

Reflection Questions
1) When have you laughed at the possibility of a situation or event? Describe it.

2) List some situations or circumstances in your life, community, and world that seem to be beyond all hope. What makes each one seem hopeless?

3) How can you specifically apply the principles of this reverse meditation to a situation or circumstance listed above?

Activity

Select one item on your hopeless list. Apply the principles of reverse meditation—frame it, insulate yourself from doubters, touch it, follow up—for at least two weeks (time will vary depending on issue). Journal your experiences daily. Meditation verse can be repeated through the day.

Meditation Verse

Not dead, just asleep.

Post-Meditation Questions

1) What issue did you choose and why?

2) What was the most difficult aspect about this meditation?

3) What were the results of this meditation?

Chapter 6
Church Reverse Meditation

Acts 20:7-12

When you visualize many stories in the Bible, the mental images you receive can be entertaining or just plain bizarre. Visualize the account about Elisha and the youth.[1] Elisha was walking and a group of young persons began teasing him and calling him "Baldhead." Elisha cursed the troublemakers and then two bears attacked the young people. Wow, Elisha was a prophet who was very sensitive about his hair loss.

Visualize the story of Balaam riding his donkey.[2] Balaam was riding his donkey and suddenly the donkey saw an angel with a sword drawn. The donkey pulled off the road to avoid the angel. Balaam never saw the angel and therefore struck his donkey for the seemly sporadic behavior. After Balaam punished the donkey two more times for avoiding this angry angel, the donkey had enough and asked Balaam why he was being so abusive. Even the donkey from Shrek would laugh at that biblical story.

Visualize Adam and Eve after their terrible mistake.[3] They ate the forbidden fruit and realized they were naked. Once they heard God approaching, they hid! They tried to hide from God! Where did they think they could go and God could not see them? Hide and seek is not a game most people should play with a being who is Omnipresent (present everywhere) and Omniscient (all-knowing).

The account of Paul and Eutychus certainly qualifies for my entertaining Bible stories list. Eutychus, a young man, sat in the balcony listening to the apostle Paul preach. Paul preached so long that the young man went to sleep, then fell a few stories to the ground. Onlookers believed the boy had died. This story takes being bored to death to a new level.

What is particularly interesting about this story is what causes this young man's demise. Eutychus was not in the midst of a heated argument that turned violent. He was not engaged in criminal activity and reaping the consequences from it. He was not at the wrong place at the wrong time, like so many young people who die prematurely. No, he was in church in the wee hours of the night.

The cause of his presumed death could be partially attributed to the church service he attended and specifically the boring sermon he attempted to hear. This may sound like a stretch to some. However, if Eutychus had not been in church, he would have never fallen off the balcony and been pronounced dead. If Eutychus was in church and the service was stimulating enough to keep him awake, he would have never fallen asleep and fallen off the balcony. The church service led the young man to sleep and his sleep led to a supposed death.

Many times, activities or organizations that are created for healthy and noble purposes produce unhealthy and destructive effects. The concept of school as place for learning possesses a healthy and noble purpose. Yet sometimes the way schools operate produces a disdain for learning among children and adults. Family reunions can keep extended family members connected. They can serve as a time of renewal and a preservation of tradition. Yet sometimes family reunions produce strife and stress.

Similar to the concept of school or a family reunion, the purpose behind the existence of the Church is pure. We can even say it is holy. Yet our "execution" of church often causes pain, resentment and indifference to people both inside and outside the Church. The Church sometimes leads people to enter into unhealthy meditative states.

The Goal

Many of us can relate to Eutychus. We tried to do the right thing. We were in church. We were in the "right" place. But the Church led us into a state or position that was worst than when we entered. We came to church seeking encouragement and we left with a bitter taste in our mouths. We came to church because someone else convinced us that we must go and we left with more reasons why we should not return. We came to church to be restored and we left broken. These unpleasant encounters can lead to spiritual apathy or various forms of spiritual death, where hope ceases to live. *Church Reverse Meditation attempts to bring people out of the negative meditative states that the church has triggered.*

Negative Meditation

There were certain conditions that led to Eutychus' detrimental meditative state. The lack of focus and practicality in the worship experience that Eutychus encountered contributed to his negative state. This negative meditative state occurs in conjunction with his sleep.

Purpose of Worship

The purpose of the gathering that Eutychus attended was clear. The people were in the house to celebrate the Lord's Supper. Since Paul had reached his last day with the people, he decided to preach to them throughout the night. The primary purpose behind the gathering became secondary. The communion of the people and their remembrance of Christ's sacrifice became secondary to Paul's sermon.

So often in the church we get sidetracked. We give major focus to minor things, and those minor things drive many people away from the church. I have been to Bible studies where visitors were recognized, announcements were made, pastor's comments were made and an offering was taken, and not one prayer was uttered. I have been to services that lasted so long, one of the preachers for the evening had to leave due to another obligation. I have sat in services that had so many activities, speakers, dancers and songs that I forgot the theme or purpose behind the service.

Sometimes going to church is similar to going to the movies. I love going to the movies. Almost each time I go, I get a bag of popcorn and a medium Sprite. I find my seat and I wait for the lights to dim. The screen lights up and announcements are made to turn off cell phones. A plug or two for the movie theater is given. The coming attractions start. After about the fifth movie preview, I turn to my wife and ask her, "What movie did we come to see again?" A lot of times people come into our worship services, Bible studies or church activities and they ask the same question. "What exactly did I come to this church for?" Many churches are consumed with minor things. When unchurched people see where our focus is, they question the overall purpose for our existence.

Some might read this passage in Acts and say that Paul was not doing something minor. He was preaching the Word of God, which is a major, important activity in the Church. This is without a doubt true. However, when a good thing is done too long or done at the wrong time, often it loses its effectiveness.

I had a professor in college who had a wonderful rule about the length of papers. When a student would ask him how long the paper had to be, he would always respond, "The paper should be long enough so that you can complete the assignment well." What a beautiful way to put it. Write a paper that is long enough to fulfill your task, nothing more and nothing less. Just get the job done.

A lot of times, the church allows its customs and traditions to dictate when a service or activity should end instead of basing the activity or service on when it has fulfilled its purpose. Some churches will worship for two and half hours every Sunday, even if some Sundays everyone could be spiritually fed in one and a half hours. Some churches will worship for an hour every Sunday, even if some Sundays the Spirit is moving the congregation to be in worship for an hour and twenty minutes. Do it until the job is done—nothing more and nothing less.

Practicality of Worship

The length of time that Paul spent preaching also infringed on people's bodily needs. No matter how great and dynamic a preacher may be, very few, if any, can keep a large group's attention for hours on end late at night. The more I mature as a pastor, the more sensitive I become to the practicality of worship.

Before I began serving in pastoral ministry full-time, I adamantly believed the sermon was the most important part of Sunday morning worship. I thought a powerful preacher could grow any ministry, could captivate any uninterested, tired soul and could even move mountains. Once I started to serve as a pastor, I began to realize how many practical issues could deflate the power of the preached moment. A noisy air conditioner can deflate the preached moment, or a broken air conditioner on a hot summer day can distract the most astute listener. A church full of hearing aids and a poor sound system can take the wind out of the best preacher's sail. Preaching a sermon in a different location than what the congregation is accustomed to can frustrate the you-know-what out of people. I had a woman tell me, "Every time you preach, I can't hear a word you say because you walk around and don't preach from the pulpit." There is a practical aspect to worship that must be addressed, because if it is ignored the worship experience will suffer.

There is also a possibility that Paul's speaking was pushing back dinner for at least some gathered in the house. We must remember that the Lord's Supper in the first century church was much closer to an actual meal than our twenty-first century version of it. In Paul's letter to the Corinthians, he scolded them for treating the Lord's Supper too much like an ordinary meal: "When you come together, it is not the Lord's Supper you eat, for as you eat, each of you goes ahead without waiting for anybody else. One remains hungry, another gets drunk. Don't you have homes to eat and drink in?"[4] Paul's outrage reveals one interesting aspect about the Lord's Supper in Corinth: sometimes people ate and drank enough for it to serve as their actual supper. Paul warned the believers against using the Lord's Supper to fill their stomachs, but Paul's warning revealed what was practiced among some believers. For the ones who did not fall asleep, like Eutychus, they could have been experiencing hunger pains based on their expectation of receiving a meal that night (or at least a snack).

I am certainly not suggesting that we become slaves to convenience and luxury, but all church leaders must be sensitive to where possible distractions could arise. All worship services, studies or church activities must follow Jesus' lead and be attentive to people's spiritual and physical needs. Jesus was a master of sensing the spiritual as well as the natural needs of others. After Jesus healed and taught a crowd of more than 5,000 people in an isolated place, his disciples came to him. They advised Jesus to send the people back to their towns, so that they could purchase food. The disciples believed the people received what they came for and now they should depart. Yet Jesus was sensitive to the distance that they would have to travel on empty stomachs and responded to his disciples, "They do not need to go away. You give them something to eat."[5] Jesus was in tune with his followers' spiritual and physical needs.

Paul's lengthiness and insensitivity to the congregation's bodily needs turned the Word into merely words. Eutychus no longer heard and felt the living, active breath of God, but he heard a multiplicity of words, which led him into a deadly sleep.

I have become an eyewitness to how the church has become an accomplice in its own demise. We, the Church, are partially responsible for many of the negative meditative states among our young and old. Our inflexibility, our fear of change, our dogged commitment to ritualism and traditions more often than not trumps practicality, common sense and seeing the writing on the wall. The results are a loss of respect for the church and a continual reflection on all the negative aspects of it. Just as Eutychus fell, many people's veneration for the church fell based on church people's actions.

Reverse Meditation

Through an examination of Paul's response to Eutychus, we receive some insight into the practice of Church Reverse Meditation. First and foremost, we must regard the fact that Paul responded as significant. Paul was at least partially liable for Eutychus' demise and took responsibility for Eutychus' restoration.

There is a cliché that many use to end a relationship: "It is not you; it is me." This line expresses that the problem in the relationship is not the "other" person, but the initiator of the break-up, "me." Church Reverse Meditation starts from the simple premise that it is not the world, but it is the church that is the problem. Everyone in the church needs to say, "It is not the world; we are the reason why our pews are not filled and communities are not transformed."

The Church is quick to cite all the reasons why people are jaded or indifferent to joining the Body of Christ. Many times, the finger is pointed outward. "People are not as respectful as they used to be." "People used to respect the church; now they don't even care." "This world is going crazy." "Our youth are so lost." "That neighborhood is not safe anymore."

When is the Church going to take responsibility for the current state of the world? When is the Church going to admit that it focused on the construction of new edifices, but neglected the people? When is the church going to admit that having more financial security started to compete with customized local outreach and mission? When is the church going to admit that it became more comfortable with talking about Jesus to Christians than to non-Christians? When is the church going to admit that evangelism became an archaic word? When is the church going to say to the world, "It's not you, world; it's us?"

This form of reverse meditation starts with an acknowledgement that the Church is part of the problem. *It involves serious reflection on the role that the Church plays in its own demise.* When a person recognizes his or her wrongdoing, a posture of humility and openness is easier to take. This is the exact posture the Church needs to possess with the world.

The text informs us that Paul wraps himself around the young man. The importance of physical contact has already been mentioned in the previous chapter and is also significant here. The type of physical contact that Paul made was an embrace. Paul surrounded the boy with his presence.

People outside the body of Christ, especially our young people, deserve our utmost attention. We must become like the father of the prodigal son, running out and showering the lost son with our presence and concern. We must be there for them.

Sometimes the best thing that we can do is simply be present for someone. We do not always need to find the "right" scripture, say the perfect prayer, or have the awe-inspiring advice. Simply being present for someone is an underestimated quality. Often the greatest comfort that we can find as human beings is not from words or grandiose deeds, but from just knowing that someone will be present throughout our storms and trials. Can you simply be there for a person outside the body of Christ? Can you be still and wait for the person to realize God's grace through your unwavering presence? *This form of reverse meditation requires being present with those*

who do not yet believe or are confused. Your presence among the unsaved will facilitate your reflection on the Church's shortcomings.

Lastly, Paul proclaimed to the congregation that Eutychus was alive. Paul spoke words of encouragement concerning the boy to the congregation.

How often in the church do we hear about the problems of the world? We hear about the declining state of the world and its loss of morals. We hear about all that is going wrong. Identifying problems is not detrimental. Yet some churches seem to focus on problems and even enjoy it. We can never forget that we are not in the gloom and doom business. We are in the hope business as the church. Regardless of your theological sensibilities, the hope and power from Jesus' resurrection is undeniable. That light can never be overshadowed by the darkness of the world.

You cannot proclaim that light and hope is visible in the world unless you see it yourself. You cannot see that light and hope with your natural eyes; you must look with your eyes of faith. To see with your eyes of faith means to trust in God's revelation. If you take time out to be still and silent with God, he will open your eyes to some things you never noticed before.

Every morning, I get up, go into my closet, shut the door, sit on the floor, light a candle and do absolutely nothing. I simply sit there and close my eyes. Sometimes my mind is racing and sometimes it is focused. Sometimes I employ some specific centering techniques and other times I am not as disciplined. Sometimes I am in there for 40 minutes and other times seven minutes. The one thing that stays the same is that I go and sit there every day.

One morning, my mind was flooded by all that I needed to do in the church and all that was not working the way I wanted. (These thoughts had frequently infringed upon my time for at least six months.) While these thoughts flooded my head, some foreign, alien thoughts—distinct from the rest— emerged. "There are at least ten new people who have started attending your church over the last year." "Two people have given their lives to Christ since you have been there." The moment was literally amazing. I said to myself, "Wow, I had never thought about that before."

Everything that emerged in my consciousness that morning were facts that I already knew. Some of them were even facts that people had told me before, but I could not see them. They had to be revealed to me. I was looking with my natural eyes, and all I could see was what was going wrong. My moments in the closet helped me to open my eyes of faith.

God reveals the beauty and all that is right with the world to us in many different ways. I offered an example of one way that worked for me. Once the awesomeness of the world is revealed, the same question awaits us all: What will you do with this new insight? *Church Reverse Meditation moves you to reflect continually upon all that is beautiful in the world and to become vessels for others to see God's awesomeness.*

Results of Church Reverse Meditation
The transformation in Paul's approach from the beginning of the evening is highlighted in the linguistic shift the author of Acts makes. In verse seven, the Greek word used to describe Paul's activity was *dialegomai*. This word is translated as "preached,"[6] "spoke,"[7] "talking,"[8] and "lectured."[9] The first definition for this Greek word in *The Strongest Strong's*

Exhaustive Concordance is "to reason."[10] From the various renderings of this word, coupled with the context clues observed from the text, one could assume that Paul was talking to (or even talking at) the people, not with them.

After Eutychus had been identified as alive, a different word is used for Paul's activity in verse eleven: *homileo*. The King James Version, New American Standard Bible, and The New International Version all translate this word as talked or talking. Greek scholar Alfred Marshall translates the word as "conversing."[11] *The Expository Dictionary of Bible Words* defines homileo as "talked with," or "discussed."[12]

Homileo is used two times in the road to Emmaus account.[13] The word is used to describe the conversation that two men were having before Jesus interrupted them. In Acts 24:26, the word is used to describe the communication that occurred between Felix and Paul when Paul was imprisoned. In the accounts of Emmaus and Paul and Felix, *homileo* is used in a context where there is explicit interaction and mutual exchange.

When Paul first entered the house, he preached, reasoned and lectured the people, but after Eutychus woke up, he entered into a conversation with the people. He talked with them. He conversed with them. An interaction between him and the people occurred, where before there were only directives and speeches. After Paul attended to Eutychus, he began to commune with the people.

The body of Christ is a community. When we gather and attention is not given to fostering and strengthening that bond, we begin to undermine our church's existence. Worship, Bible studies, and church activities should bring us closer together. We should be tighter and stronger from coming together, not beaten down and tired. Church Reverse Meditation will produce a more attentive church and church leaders who are sensitive to the voices and needs of the people inside and outside of the Church. This form of reverse meditation should lead to more conversation and openness within the Church. If the church is going to grow deeper and stronger, we do not simply need more sermons, more doctrine or more reasons why we should follow Christ. We need genuine communion and connection with each other.

Prayer
Precious Lord, just as your body was broken, so do we reside in a broken church. Our pastors are imperfect. Our members sometimes lack faithfulness. Your most fundamental command to love others often goes unheeded. Yet brokenness can lead to strength, when we surrender to you. We acknowledge our shortcomings. Please help your church, God. Amen.

How to Awake with God

Review
Goal: Break negative meditative states that the church triggered.

Negative Meditation: Reflections about the shortcomings and uncertain priorities of the Church.

Reverse Meditation:
- Reflect on the role that the church plays in its demise.
- Being present with those who do not yet believe or are confused.
- Become a vessel for others to see God's awesomeness.

Reflections questions
1) Can you think of a moment when the church let you down or disappointed you? Why were you disappointed? What should have been done differently in that situation?

2) What are some common causes that prevent the body of Christ from functioning as it should?

3) List a few reasons why your family members or friends do not go to church. What can be done on your part and the church's part to change that?

Activity

If Christ were to walk into your church each day of the week, what would make him smile, what would make him upset and what would he be indifferent to? Create a list with a column for each category (smiles, frowns, and indifference). Pick one aspect from each list.

Begin to reflect on how you can make Jesus smile, eliminate what would make Jesus frown, and deemphasize what Jesus would be indifferent to. This meditative process would also be beneficial to practice with a group, so that change within a particular church can start to move forward.

Meditation Verse
Catch us Lord, for we have fallen.

Post-Meditation Questions

1) Which item did you pick from each column and why?

2) Where do you see the greatest potential for change in your church?

3) How can you help to implement sustainable change in your church?

Chapter 7
Escape Reverse Meditation

Jonah 1:1-2:1

At one time or another, you may have heard the phrase "they are running from their calling." Growing up in my church, I heard this phrase applied to people who had the graces and gifts for pastoral ministry, but did not pursue the vocation. This phrase was repeated even more as I worked my way through the ordination process of the United Methodist Church. Many pastors revealed how they stopped running from their calling and began the journey toward pastoral ministry. The phrase in the Church often indicates a person's resistance to a divinely given task.

Although running from your calling is not a positive activity, the phrase usually indicates certain positive qualities about the person to whom it is applied. First, the phrase indicates that the person is gifted enough to be called by God to do something. God trusts this person enough to give him or her a divine task. Second, it indicates that the person has the spiritual sensibilities to know that they are being called. One cannot run from a calling he or she has never heard. To hear a calling from God reveals a level of spiritual discernment and maturity that many people do not have. In some ways, to say that a person is running from his or her calling is a backward compliment.

However a person who runs from his or her calling is regarded, nothing should overshadow that person's ignorance (and I mean this in the most benign way). Running away from God is impossible. A person once told me there are only two directions you can move: Either you can move toward God or you can move toward God. When people think they are moving away from God, they trip over God as they run out the back door. Why do you think people find God in the strangest places? Why do you think some people encounter God in dark alleys, drug-infested neighborhoods or war zones? Why do you think some people encounter God when they are smothered in materialism or hedonism or anguish? The answer is simple, but the implications are beyond our mental capacity: *God is everywhere.*

Running from God is similar to running on a treadmill. No matter how fast you run, how long you run or how hard you run on that treadmill, when you finally stop, you will be in the same place. Likewise with God, no matter how fast you run, how long you run or how hard you run, when you finally stop, you will still be in a place where God resides. You can run from God, but you can never run and get away from God. Unfortunately, some people learn this lesson the hard way. The prophet Jonah is a prime example of a person who learns the difficult way that running away from his calling is not an option.

The Goal

Though Jonah headed in the opposite direction from where God wanted him to go, he still had divine encounters along his journey. These experiences eventually turned Jonah around and launched him in the direction God intended for him. The purpose behind Escape Reverse Meditation is inspired by Jonah's turn-around. The goal of this meditation is to redirect us from escaping from God so we can intentionally pursue God's beckoning. This form of reverse meditation brings us out of the meditative state of stubbornness—a constant reflection on how we will not follow God's lead.

Negative Meditation

God gave Jonah an assignment to go to Nineveh, but Jonah decided to go in a different direction. Imagine Jonah's situation. Jonah received his divine assignment, then he reflected on how much he did not want to go or why going would be useless. He reflected on how much he resented the people and place he was being sent to. He reflected on how much he resented his task and how much of an inconvenience it would be. He began to meditate on how much he did not want to do it and all the reasons why he should not do it. He eventually placed himself in a meditative state of stubbornness. This stubbornness culminated with Jonah going to sleep. A few circumstances set the stage for Jonah to be lulled into this negative meditative state.

Role of Prophet

Stubbornness was a common occupational hazard of Jonah's profession as a prophet. God summoned prophets to point out what was neglected, forgotten or flawed among individuals or societies. Throughout the Bible, prophets were almost always rejected at least once. Prophets were ridiculed, persecuted and even killed. Prophets experienced these difficulties for one simple reason: no one liked to hear about their faults. When a major part of your job is to point out faults, you can expect to receive a lot of abuse and criticism.

At the beginning of many pastors' careers, they strongly identify with the role of the prophet. They want to be agents of change in the church. They want to expose the dark spots in the church and move to richer, more spirit-filled experiences. They want to challenge the church to serve the community instead of themselves and to love more whole-heartedly. They want to deemphasize committees and "power families" and allow God's spirit to take the lead.

A few years in ministry teach many pastors that the role of the prophet in the church is a role that will cause much emotional abuse for them. They discover that being a prophet may lead to less people in worship service. They discover that being a prophet may lead to yelling matches in committee meetings and looks that could kill from parishioners. They discover that being a prophet may lead to members circumventing their authority and reaching out to former pastors to bury their loved ones. They discover that being a prophet can make the church (as bad as it may sound) a miserable place to be. So many pastors slowly move further and further away from the role of the prophet because the abuse and turmoil are more than they can bear.

Jonah was acutely aware of the insults, rejection, abuse and turmoil that come from being a prophet. He was aware that this negativity could intensify ten-fold with people who had been accustomed to doing things their way for a long time. All the suffering that Jonah would have to endure consumed his mind.

Focus
Refusal to do God's will become inevitable when you focus on all that you will lose. This is a common scenario among people called into pastoral ministry from another career. They receive a call from God and then focus on how much their salary will decrease in ministry. They focus on how

much money they will spend by going to seminary. They focus on how much time it will take to make the transition. They focus on how their relationships might change or be severed because of their call. Their focus on all that they will lose causes them to stay put and rationally oppose where God is calling them.

When these same people shift their focus from what they will lose to all they will gain, the transition to go with God becomes much easier. They focus on all the joy and fulfillment they will gain in ministry. They focus on all they will learn during their time in seminary. They focus on how much they will grow spiritually and emotionally during their transition. They focus on all the new relationships that they will make. When they focus on all that they have to gain, responding to God's call seems more like an exciting adventure than a laborious chore.

What if Jonah had focused on all that he could have gained by following God instead of all that he would have lost? There is little evidence to suggest that Jonah switched or broadened his focus from what he would lose. He focused on the difficulties of his divine task, which set him on a course for a meditative state of stubbornness.

Jonah coupled his selective focus with movement. The Scriptures describe that Jonah flees from the Lord. A person flees from people or situations that he or she believes are harmful. As a result of Jonah being focused on the difficulties of his divine task, he began to treat the Lord as a person who wanted to hurt him.

Rash Action

Jonah's limited focus led to rash actions. Sometimes the best action that you can take in a situation that is troubling is to do nothing. When an assignment, role or circumstance confronts you that seems problematic, be still for a moment. A little silence and a little stillness can go a long way. If Jonah had stood still for a moment after he received his assignment, then he could have possibly gained a greater perspective on the assignment. He could have realized some of the gains that could occur through this divine task.

Missed Connection

Jonah also neglected to make the connection between the strong winds that were disturbing his boat and his refusal to fulfill his divine task. Many people commonly mistake spiritual resistance for divine punishment. God has established a divine order. All have places in that order and were designed to fit in that order in particular ways. When we are unaware of that structure or decide to intentionally go against that structure, we will experience spiritual friction. We naively label this friction as problems, trials or even divine punishment, but it is actually the normal cosmological backlash that occurs when we attempt to circumvent or adapt God's order.

For example, if you have a round peg and you desire to put that round peg in a square hole, it will not fit. You will have difficulty placing it into the hole. You may hurt your hand. You may damage the peg or hole. None of the difficulties, injuries or frustrations that you experience are personal attacks against you. They are just the natural repercussions of trying to perform an action that was not intended to be performed.

The same is true in our lives. God shaped us in certain ways. God intends for us to choose from certain paths. When we choose to ignore God's blueprints, to do other things, or go in different directions, we experience difficulties. Those difficulties are not divine punishment; they are spiritual friction.

Jonah experienced spiritual friction. He was designed and called to speak repentance to a nation, but he chose to remain silent. He was designed and called to interact with people, but he chose to turn away from people. He was designed and called to confront, but he chose to avoid. He was designed and called to be bold, but he chose to be timid. He was designed and called to be a prophet in a nation, but he chose to be a passenger on a boat. Each time Jonah tried to fit the shape of a prophet into the hole of a passenger, he experienced friction.

Do not be so quick to blame God for difficulties you are experiencing. Maybe you are designed and called to do something that is incompatible with where you are. Maybe you are forcing a relationship, job, career, major, or living arrangement into a hole that does not fit. Maybe you need to spend some time with your Creator in prayer, meditation, church fellowship, and fasting to clarify what exactly your shape and size is, and where it will be compatible.

Jonah focused on all that he would lose by going to Nineveh. He ran away instead of being still. He ignored the spiritual friction that his actions caused. In order to prevent his mind or spirit from convicting him to repent, he entered into a meditative state of stubbornness. He found a spot on the boat and went to sleep.

Reverse Meditation

Although Jonah was intent on sleeping, God was intent on waking him up. Jonah's negative meditative state was broken by several opportunities that came his way. The captain asked Jonah to pray to God. He petitioned Jonah to practice his faith. This scenario is very interesting. A person unfamiliar with Yahweh requested that a prophet of Yahweh pray.

Sometimes the loudest calls to exercise faith come from those who have little or no professed faith themselves. When I was admitted into college, I had the opportunity to start attending classes a semester early and become acclimated to the campus. I had a roommate who was a nominal believer. He observed me every morning as I rose and said my prayers beside my bed.

When the fall semester came, we decided to room together again. In the fall, I changed my prayer routine. I began praying once I got out of the shower and doing my devotions in the bathroom. Midway through the semester, my roommate asked me, "Why don't you pray anymore, like you did before? What happened?" I was shocked at his question and a little offended by the underlying suggestion that I had become spiritually complacent. I do not remember my response, but it was one cloaked in defensiveness.

As I reflected back on his question, it served a vital function in my life. It challenged me to examine whether I was using the light of Christ to impact my college environment or allowing my college environment to adversely impact me. Looking back, he could have been right. I might have slacked off spiritually, but even more shocking was the fact that he cared. He held me accountable, even though his prayer life was nonexistent.

Everyone needs at least a few people around them that will, as the saying goes, "tell it like it is." Often what keeps us in negative meditative states are family, friends and acquaintances who refuse to challenge us and hold us accountable. Healthy relationships find the balance between confrontation and comfort. Escape Reverse Meditation involves using networks and systems that keep us accountable to the faith that we profess. *This form of reverse meditation moves us to reflect upon how or if we are practicing our faith in the present.*

Jonah had another opportunity that helped break his meditative state. He had the chance to give his testimony to the people on the boat. After the sailors determined that Jonah knew the cause of the storm, they asked him about his background and life. Jonah answered by saying, "I am a Hebrew and I worship the Lord, the God of heaven, who made the sea and the land."[1] As Jonah began to tell the sailors about Yahweh and himself, I believe he started to realize the absurdity of his plans to escape from God's call. Jonah tells the sailors that his God is the God of the sea, but he attempts to run from this God by traveling across the sea.

Sometimes just proclaiming who God is can redirect you from inevitable failure. Simply stating that God is creator of all can redirect you from acting as if you own anything. Simply stating that God's time is not your time can redirect you from being fixated on time tables. Simply stating that God is the source of all wisdom can redirect you from thinking you know what is best. Simply stating that God is ruler can redirect you from thinking you are in control. Preaching God's Word to other people often convicts and redirects me in some of the places I am moving towards.

Never underestimate the power of the proclaimed Word. *Escape Reverse Meditation employs self-reminders in order to break us out of spiritual stupors.* Sometimes we will not do the things that we want to do unless we are reminded. Sometimes there is no one around to remind us, so we must figure out a way to remind ourselves. We can write a note and place it in a strategic place. We can set cell phones, timers and alarms. We can record messages. We remind ourselves about what must be done.

By Jonah proclaiming what he believed, he was able to see with greater clarity the folly of his plans. Living a life of faith is the same way. There are certain actions that must be taken; there are certain attitudes and mindsets that must be adopted. Sometimes the preacher is not going to be around to give you a powerful Word. Sometimes your prayer partner will be unavailable. Sometimes your spiritual friend will be occupied. In those moments you must find ways to remind yourself and encourage yourself about what must be done as a person of faith.

Jonah had a final opportunity to break out of his meditative state. He sacrificed himself for the people on the boat. He took a risk for the benefit of others. There is nothing better to break you out of a stubborn meditative state than to do something for someone else.

My mother has a great saying: "If you ever are feeling down and depressed about how life is treating you, go do something for someone else and you will feel a lot better." We can get so consumed by what is happening in our life that we literally suffocate on our own "issues." The remedy to the situation is a breath of fresh air or, in other words, a break from thinking about ourselves. The best way to stop thinking about yourself is to do something for someone else.

Jonah gave himself a break from his issues. For the entire trip, Jonah had been pouting about being a prophet. He had been thinking about how horrible his life was going to be in a place where he was not welcomed. He was mulling over in his head all the abuse he had taken. He was convincing himself of all the reasons why he should not go and would not go to Nineveh. In the midst of all his worrying, complaining and self-pity, Jonah never took time to consider that other people around him were suffering. Once Jonah took the focus off himself and recognized the plight of others, he was able to make a sacrifice for the good of the ship.

Escape Reverse Meditation moves us to move for others. It propels us to take risks with others' interests and concerns in mind. *This meditation involves intentional reflection on other people's plights instead of our own.* This will in many cases lead to a softening of a stubborn stance.

Swallowed Up

After Jonah threw himself out of the ship "the Lord provided a great fish to swallow [*bala*]"[2] him. The Hebrew word *bala* is often used to indicate one who has been devoured or destroyed. In Pharaoh's dream, in the book of Genesis, seven skinny heads of grain swallowed up (*bala*) seven full heads of grain.[3] In the book of Exodus, Aaron's rod swallowed up (*bala*) the rods of Pharaoh's servants.[4] In the book of Numbers, the Earth swallowed up (*bala*) the Israelite rebel Korah for his sins.[5] *Bala* is frequently used to indicate the termination of life or the conclusion. In contrast, Jonah was swallowed up (*bala*), but not destroyed. He was covered by the mouth of a fish, but not devoured. In Jonah's darkest moment, there was still light. In his lowest point, Jonah still had hope. God was not finished with him yet!

The end is never the end when you are with God. There will be times when you are thrown overboard to die. There will be moments when all rescue attempts have seemed to fail. There will be times when all plans and efforts for redemption have faded away. There will be times when you have been defeated and oppressed. In those moments, remember that you may have been swallowed up, but you have not been destroyed.

Second Chance

Jonah received not just any second chance, but a divine second chance. He is an example of what makes second chances from God special. Jonah 3:1 tells us that God came and spoke to Jonah a second time. God spoke the same thing to Jonah the first time that he did the second time. The difference between the first and second time was not God's Word, but Jonah's reaction to it.

God always gives us a second chance to respond to his Word. God's Word does not change. What changes is our attitudes toward his Word and our understandings of it. So often we are like teenagers that reject their parents' advice for years. Later, as we mature and become adults, we realize how helpful our parents' counsel is. Their counsel has not changed, but we have grown to a point where we can value it.

Chapter three reveals another second chance given to Jonah. Even though Jonah went to a place God did not command him to go, Jonah's destination did not change. His location changed, but his destination stayed the same. There are some places that God calls you to that will never change. There are some places from which you simply cannot run. God will call you to those places until you arrive there or until your dying day.

God also granted Jonah a second chance to accomplish an important task. God did not demote Jonah for his disobedience and send him to a less significant city. The Nineveh assignment was still as great and important as when Jonah was first given it. The great thing about God is that God's assignments do not depreciate over time. If God desired that you do something, 5 days, 5 months, 5 years or even 50 years ago, then that assignment is as valuable and important today. There are some divine assignments that do not have expiration dates on them. You will never be at peace until you do what God has desired you to do.

Lastly, God gave Jonah a second chance to be relevant. Though Jonah rejected God's command the first time, God still allowed Jonah to participate in helping other people and impacting their lives in a positive way. If you have breath in your lungs, then God can use you in a meaningful way for others' benefit. God always gives you a second chance to be relevant in other people's lives and for their good. Even though you may have hurt someone's feelings, God gives you a second chance to heal. Even though you may have spoken harshly to someone, God gives you a second chance to uplift. Even though you may have robbed someone of an opportunity or treated him or her poorly, God gives you a second chance to act justly. Even though you may have ignored someone, God gives you a second chance to offer your undivided attention. Even though you may have denied someone, God gives you a second chance to embrace and accept someone. God always offers us a second chance to do good in spite of all the times we did wrong.

Conclusion

When we think about all the times we did not get something right, we should be thankful for second chances. When we think about all the mishaps we made in school, the assignments we forgot to submit, papers that we didn't write so well, the test that we failed, we should be so thankful that some teachers said, "I am going to drop this lowest score." When we think about the relationships we messed up, the friendships we fumbled, or the bridges we burned, we should be so thankful that someone said, "I am going to forgive you." When we think about all the mistakes we have made, the times we misspoke, the moments we offered an unkind gesture, we should be so thankful that some people said, "I am going to give them the benefit of the doubt, they were having a rough day." When we think about our lack of stewardship over what God has entrusted to us, how we don't eat healthy foods, exercise like we should, use our financial resources compassionately, or use our skills for more people's benefit, we should be so thankful that we can say, "I still have a body, resources, skills and abilities to use for God's glory."

We should be thankful for second chances we received by God's grace.

Your darkest hour marks the end of your negative meditation. It marks the point of your u-turn. It marks the beginning of your second chance. It marks the point when you reverse your course and heed the direction God has set for you. It is the moment when you realize that there is no escape from God's call on your life.

Prayer

Holy God, thank you for never leaving us, even when we have tried to escape you. May your omnipresent nature become a benefit to us, not a burden. May we run to you, not run away from you. Allow your grace to be experienced through our obedience. So be it.

How to Awake with God

Review

Goal: Break the meditative state of stubbornness.

Negative Meditation:

- Reflect on how and why you should not follow God.
- Focus on the disadvantages of following God.
- Rash action.
- Missing the connection between the physical and spiritual.

Reverse Meditation:

- Reflect upon how or if you are practicing your faith in the present.
- Employ self-reminders in order to break out of spiritual stupors.
- Reflect on other people's plights instead of your own.

Reflection

1) Have you ever run from something or someone who had your best interest in mind? If so, why?

2) What do you believe God has called or is calling you to do? How have you responded to that call?

3) What do you fear most about responding to God's call?

Activity

Find an open space in your home. Turn toward a window that is bearing light. Kneel down and prostrate yourself. As you lay prostrate, say the meditation verse. Repeat five to ten times. After you are done, sit quietly for at least five minutes. Allow the Spirit to convict you on all the things that you have not surrendered to the Lord.

Meditation Verse

I surrender, Lord.

Post-Meditation Questions

1) What has God revealed to you that you have yet to surrender?

2) Why is surrendering difficult for you?

3) What Scriptures affirm your need to surrender?

Chapter 8
Fate Reverse Meditation

Acts 12:1-11

As a young boy, I aspired to become a lawyer. I read about the legal system. I watched every court drama possible. From all my inquiries, what fascinated me the most was the concept of reasonable doubt. I discovered that a defense attorney's primary job was to expose doubt regarding the claim against an accused person. Just one reasonable doubt could get a person off the hook for committing a crime.

Almost two decades later, I see that there is a reverse parallel between the legal system and the spiritual realm. In the spiritual realm, just one doubt can cause you to miss your blessing. In the Bible there is story after story where people have missed their blessings because of doubt. God positioned them perfectly to be blessed, but their doubts messed it up. God tracked them to be convicted to a life of abundance, joy and fulfillment, but the reasonable doubts raised sent them back home to ordinary lives.

A group of people said to Jesus, "We want to believe that you are the Messiah, but we have some doubts. Miraculously produce some bread, feed us and then we will believe." Jesus responded, "You missed your blessing because I am the bread. You could have been feasting on me all along."[1]

When Jesus returned to his hometown to teach and heal friends, family and associates, they responded, "We don't believe that you are all that everyone says you are. We grew up with you and knew your mother and daddy." Jesus could only perform a few miracles because of their doubts.[2] When the disciple Thomas refused to believe his colleagues about Jesus' resurrection, Thomas' doubts caused him to miss the blessings of the good news.[3] When a thief on a cross doubted Jesus' divinity and power and mocked him, he squandered his seat in paradise.[4] Time and time again, we read about blessings falling to the way side because of people's doubts.

Negative Meditation

The book of Acts shows us the paralyzing effect doubt can have on a person. Herod Aggripa persecuted the church, captured and executed Christians. Peter watched friends and associates suffer or die at Herod's hand. In Acts 12, Peter finds himself in a similar situation. He was imprisoned at Herod's command and awaited a trial. The likelihood that Peter would be persecuted or executed was high. In the midst of these circumstances and reflections, Peter goes to sleep. Reminders of the fellow Christians who had suffered and died surrounded Peter. He walked in the same places they walked, was captured by the same people and held in the same place. As Peter went to sleep, he meditated on his foreseeable demise. Peter was a follower of Christ and a witness to Christ's power, but signs surrounded Peter to make him doubt deliverance.

The Goal

Like Peter, we reflect on inevitable fates in our lives. When we regard a particular situation as unavoidable based on our previous experiences or observations, we have fallen asleep. When we make such evaluations we disregard the unique plan that God has for our lives.

Your fate is not sealed by the world. Just because you do not know anyone who received the job does not mean that your interview is going to produce the same results. Just because treatment did not work for the first group does not mean that your group's treatment is destined to be ineffective. Just because their relationship did not survive does not mean your relationship will do the same. Just because they did not get the support does not mean that you will not get the support. Just because they did not survive does not mean the same will be true for you. Just because that did not work for them does not mean it will not work for you.

The goal of Fate Reverse Meditation is to disrupt your reflections on the inevitable triumph of the world. This reverse meditation will cause you to consider multiple realities beside what initially appears to be certain. In the midst of failure, difficulty, pain and sorrow, this reverse meditation will bring you to say, "What God has for me is just for me no precedent, no statistic, no survey, no track record can take that away from me. I am unique in God's eyes."

Power of Prayer

Peter was in a situation that seemed inevitable. He seemed to be looking into the eyes of a cruel fate. During Peter's imprisonment "prayer was made without ceasing of the church unto God for him."[5] Often times the meditative dimension of prayer is overlooked when this verse is read. If the church was in a constant state of prayer for Peter, then that means that she constantly petitioned God for Peter's safety and release. If the church asked repeatedly for Peter's safety, then she was also in a continual state of reflection upon Peter's safety and release. The Body of Christ meditated on the release and protection of Peter while petitioning God. This set the stage for Peter's rescue.

Reverse Meditation

Peter went from being in the prison by himself with no hope and death only a few hours away to an angel present beside him eager to free him. Peter's circumstances changed in the blink of an eye. *The first step in this reverse meditation is to be ready for your circumstances to change.* You must be on the lookout for your change to come. The Bible mentions frequently the important part alertness plays in your deliverance. When Jesus' disciples asked him what will be the sign of his return, he responded,

> Therefore be on the alert, for you do not know which day your Lord is coming. But be sure of this, that if the head of the house had known at what time of the night the thief was coming, he would have been on the alert and would not have allowed his house to be broken into. For this reason you also must be ready; for the Son of Man is coming at an hour when you do not think {He will.}[6]

The disciples wanted a sure way to know the end of time was near, but Jesus told them they should be ready at all times for his return. If one is a disciple of Jesus Christ, then one lives a lifestyle which allows him or her to be ready in any moment for Christ's return.

When the angel came into Peter's cell, Peter was sleeping. He was not alert. He gave little indication that he expected anything to happen or anyone to rescue him. Peter was fortunate the angel woke him up or this would have been a short chapter.

How many times has an angel come into your cell to rescue you, but found you sleeping and then left? How many times have your circumstances changed and you did not notice it because you were not ready, alert or attentive? You did not expect anything different to happen. You slept and missed it. Spiritual alertness is a key element to seize the blessing that God has for you. You must learn how to cultivate a spirit of expectation.

So often the expectations that you have will influence and affect what you receive. When you expect to be treated with respect and make that expectation known, people are less likely to talk to you any kind of way. When you expect excellence from those that you work with, you are more likely to get it. When a teacher expects a certain standard from his or her students, the quality of work rises. The expectations that you carry in your relationships, environments, workplaces, schools, and clubs will impact how fruitful those things are for you.

Some block the blessings that God has for them with the lackluster expectations that they construct. Your pitiful expectations tell you, "It's just another Sunday morning."

It's just another day. It's just another week. It's just another Christmas season. It's just another upcoming year. But God is knocking at your door to tell you, "No, it is not just another Sunday morning. No, it is not just another day. No, it is not just another week. No, it is not just another Christmas season. No, it is not just another upcoming year. This morning, day, week, season, and year will be like nothing you have ever experienced before. If you just change your expectations you will be able to know it, too." Always be on the lookout for God's presence, insight and direction.

I read an article about a study conducted on people called super recognizers.[7] These people possessed the uncanny ability to identify faces of people they had seen once in decades. They could spot a person from their kindergarten class who is now forty. They could recognize a waiter who served them ten years ago when they were on a business trip. They can remember facial features despite time, infrequency of contact, and the transformation of people's faces. These super recognizers were contrasted with a group of people called prosopagnosics. These people had extreme difficulty recognizing people even in their immediate family. As the article contrasted the amazing ability of one group with the incredible deficiency of another, I immediately considered what the spiritual version of these people would look like.

Some people can see God's face in any situation no matter what circumstances may be covering the Divine's face. Some are able to remember God's presence no matter how much time has transpired. Some are able to see through the externalities of life and identify God. While others cannot acknowledge the presence of the Holy in their lives. They let everything and anything interfere with their sight of God. However, there is good news for spiritual prosopagnosics. Their blindness does not have to be a permanent condition. Their line of vision is obstructed by attitudes, perspectives, preconceived notions, and expectations, which can be amended. Seeing God starts with believing and expecting God to be present in your life.

Not only must you be ready for God's presence and deliverance, but you must be prepared for them. Often times people mistake readiness for preparedness. Just because someone is willing to leave a place does not mean that he or she is set to leave. Once Peter awoke, he had to make preparations for his departure. He had to put on his sandals, clothes and cloak in order to be prepared to depart. Each item that Peter put on represented a type of preparation. Peter's sandals meant that he prepared to move, while Peter's clothes meant that he prepared to interact with the public or other people. Peter's cloak had special significance. Cloaks were often used as blankets. When Peter picked up his cloak he picked up his blanket and prepared to sleep in a new location.

Fate Reverse Meditation involves making preparations to receive and fully benefit from God's presence. Some of us make no preparations to leave sad circumstance behind and then we get mad at God when we remain in them. This reverse meditation ensures that we do our part concerning our deliverance.

Fate Reverse Meditation involves consideration on what you must do to move out of undesirable circumstances. If you want to be delivered from your current fate, then ask yourself, "What preparations have I made to move, interact with new people and to rest in new places?" A person who has changed his or her immediate circumstances, circle of friends or associates, and spiritual and emotional state is a person who as changed his or her fate.

The last step in Fate Reverse Meditation is to remember that God is the gate. Bars, walls, shackles and guards kept Peter imprisoned, but in the end nothing could block him from leaving that prison. Those people and things were not the true deciders of whether Peter stayed in prison or not. God was the gate.

In our society, we have great veneration for gatekeepers. We often hear phrases such as the gatekeeper in that company, organization or place will never allow that to happen. The gatekeepers are looked at as the power brokers and decision makers in the places they reside. They are the ones that determine whether one has access or not.

However the New International Version translation of John 10 provides an interesting perspective on gatekeepers.

The passage depicts Jesus as a good shepherd. John 10:3 states, "The watchman opens the gate for him, and the sheep listen to his voice..." In some translations it will read the doorman or porter opens the gate for him, but the NIV describes the person at the gate as a watchman. From a secular perspective, one could say the NIV translation demotes the significance of the man standing at the gate from a powerful gatekeeper to a lowly watchman. This word choice is most appropriate from a spiritual perspective because the person standing at the gate does not hold the power God does.

Verse three does not say that the man at the gate liked the shepherd and therefore opened up the gate for him. It does not say that the man at the gate received a gift from the shepherd and therefore opened up the gate for him. It does not say that the man at the gate approved of how the shepherd did his job and therefore opened up the gate. No matter how the man at the gate felt about the shepherd, that gate was going to open up when he came to check on his sheep. He was not a gatekeeper in the modern sense of the word, he was simply someone who watched the gate open and close when the shepherd came and left. The Shepherd was the true decider of when the gate opened even though another man was standing beside the gate.

All doorkeepers are nothing more than watchmen. Because when God opens the door, no matter how many times they try to close it, all they can do is watch how it springs back open again. We must learn how to say, "Mister Doorman, Misses Gatekeeper, you can close the door as much as you want. But if it is a divine door that God has for me, every time you close it is going to pop back open. You can close the door five times, fifteens times, twenty times, thirty-five times, but I just want you to know that every time you close it, it is going to pop back open. And once you realize that door is not shutting, you are going to get tired and you are going to leave that door alone. Once you leave that door alone, you are going to watch me enter."

We are so focused on the person at the door. We are so focused on the doorkeepers and the gatekeepers that we forget that God is the gate. God is the door. We forget that divine doors swing on the hinges of God's grace.

There are some things that God has set aside just for you. There are certain relationships that God has for you. There are places that God desires for you to go. There are activities and encounters that God has designed for you. There are certain blessings that God has set aside specifically for you. There are certain things that God ordained us over as a shepherd or caretaker. The way that you discern what God has set aside is by observing what doors open for you. In other words, God's grace and favor will become evident when you attempt to access the things that He has set aside for you.

Fate Reverse Meditation involves constant reminders of who the ultimate decision maker and power broker is. This meditation employs daily reflection upon the omnipotence of God. Never forget that the vastness and utter pervasiveness of God trump the achievements and limited control of human beings.

Conclusion
With God all things are possible. With God the invisible becomes visible. With God the least can become the most valuable, the last can become first and the foolish can become wise. Your fate is not determined by your chains or your

prisons. Tomorrow does not have to be like today. This year does not have to be like last year. If you would like to see a new day you must ask yourself some vital questions. "Am I looking for a change to occur?" "Am I preparing for a change to happen?" "Am I focused on God's power to change any circumstance before me?" Fate Reverse Meditation awakens you so you can experience the transforming power found in Christ Jesus. May your fate be set not by your current reality, but by God's potential and expectations for you.

Prayer

God of the universe, may we find confidence even in uncertainty. Let us operate with power even when we lack earthly control. Lead us to rest in you when peace seems far away. Amen.

How to Awake with God

Review

Goal: Disrupt and counteract your reflections on the inevitability of a situation.

Negative Meditation: Reflections of the possibility and probability of your demise.

Reverse Meditation:

- Be ready for your circumstances to change.
- Consider what you must do to move out of undesirable circumstances.
- Remind yourself of who the ultimate decision maker and power broker is.

Reflection Questions

1) How does your typical responses to seemly inevitable situations resemble and differ from Peter's response in his cell?

2) Recall a time when God rescued you from an incredibly difficult situation. How did you feel?

3) Which step of Fate Reverse Meditation do you believe will be most difficult for you and why?

Activity

Select one world event that has occurred in your lifetime. (May substitute world event for a national event.) Reflect on the world and your life before the event in the morning then reflect on the world and your life after the event in the evening. Spend at least 20 minutes in each meditation session and write your reflections in a journal. Review your journal entries at the end of the week.

Meditation Verse: Open

Post Meditation Questions:

1) Which world event did you choose and why?

2) What reflections emerged about your life before and after the event?

3) How do you think God's grace was present in this world event?

Chapter 9
A Meditation of Invincibility

Judges 16:4-21

If any biblical character could fit into our 21st century celebrity culture, that person would be Samson. He had the physical attributes of the finest athletes. He had the ego and hedonistic tendencies of the most well-known rock stars. His relationships were as high profile and as short as some of our best celebrity romances. His attitude was nonchalant and playful. His ability was awe-inspiring and his character flaws were glaringly obvious—all the ingredients of which our modern stars are made.

Unfortunately, the trajectory of Samson's career was a downward one. His life is an example of the danger we face when we refuse to wake up from a negative meditative state. Though Samson is a well-known biblical figure, only three chapters in the Bible focus exclusively on his life. Samson's purpose was outlined before his birth: to begin the liberation of Israel from the Philistines.[1] His mother and father were told how to raise him: no razor to touch his head, and no wine could be consumed by him or his mother while she carried him.[2] Yet from Samson's birth until he is old enough to marry, the Scriptures say nothing about what type of life Samson lived. To gain insight about Samson's meditative state, we must engage in some responsible biblical speculation. We can make some assumptions about Samson's childhood and upbringing by examining his attitude and characteristics as an adult.

Negative Meditation

Our first look into the personality of Samson comes in Judges 14, where he demands that his parents get a Philistine wife for him. When his parents attempted to give him some marital advice, he rejected their words and repeated his demand. Samson eventually obtained his woman.

Our next look into Samson's character comes when he loses a bet. Samson killed thirty Philistines, removed their garments and then used the clothes to repay his debt. The subsequent two windows into Samson's life involve escapes from the Philistines and a single-handed victory over them.[3] In between these two accounts, Samson was on the verge of dehydration and God miraculously provided a spring for him. In each situation Samson prevailed and received what he desired.

These few occurrences are a peek into Samson's life. He led a life where very few things were denied to him, very few repercussions were ever experienced, and every situation always ended in his favor. Samson repeatedly recalled these events in his memory. He reflected on them. He relived them. He cherished them. He boasted about them. Slowly but surely, Samson entered into a state in which he was constantly meditating on his invincibility.

Circumstances Samson Could Not Overcome

Let us examine some primary factors that made this meditative state harmful. Three elements in particular transformed Samson's meditative state into a destructive one: his associations, his judgment and Delilah's persistence.

Associations

In order to grasp the significance of Samson entering into two intimate relationships with Philistine women, one must understand the divine purpose of the Philistines. Once the Israelites moved into the promise land, they were made up of an entirely new generation. This new generation of Israel did not experience the sacrifices of their forefathers and foremothers to secure the land. They did not encounter the miraculous hand of God delivering them from Egypt. They did not have to wander the wilderness and trust God to protect and provide for them. This new generation benefited from the physical and spiritual toil of past generations, but performed little labor themselves. The book of Judges reveals that nations such as the Philistines were left among the Israelites so that the Israelites could learn how to struggle and depend on God. Judges 3:1-4 reads, "Now these are the nations which the Lord left to test Israel by them (that is, all who had not experienced any of the wars of Canaan; only in order that the generation of the sons of Israel might be taught war, those who had not experienced it formerly). These nations are: the five lords of the Philistines and all the Canaanites and the Sidonians and the Hivites who lived in Mount Lebanon, from Mount Baal-hermon as far as Lebo-hamath. They were for testing Israel, to find out if they would obey the commandments of the Lord, which He had commanded their fathers through Moses."[4] The Philistines were not simply the historic and current enemies of the Israelites, they were a divine instrument whose purpose was to sharpen Israel's battle skills and strengthen their faith.

Samson in many ways treated his enemies like friends. In modern day celebrity terms, the Philistines were Samson's frienemies. A frienemy is a person who is your enemy in public, but behind closed doors your friend. Samson fought the Philistines in very public battles and confrontations, but he desired to marry them and become a part of their families.

Samson also revealed to a Philistine woman, Delilah, his Nazirite vows to God.[5] He made this Philistine woman his confidant. I had a mentor who warned me, "Be very careful about who you share your dreams with." As I matured, I realized just how wise my mentor's words were. Our aspirations, secrets and plans are very precious treasures, which must be cherished and guarded. Each time we allow someone else to view them, we make ourselves vulnerable in that moment. Dreams can be deflated. Secrets can be exposed and plans can be ridiculed all before they reach their fruition. We must be careful about whom we share our innermost selves with. Samson shared his innermost self with a person that was his enemy.

Most people say (and even Samson himself says) that the source of Samson's strength was his long hair. This is inaccurate. The source of Samson's strength was his uninterrupted commitment to God. Samson's long hair was simply the physical sign of this commitment. When Samson told Delilah the source of his strength, he allowed someone to interfere with the commitment and bond he had established with God. Samson lost his strength not because his hair was cut; he lost his strength because he allowed his relationship with Delilah to supersede his relationship with God, the source of his strength. Do you think God would have allowed Samson to become weak if he had kept his secret and Delilah just cut his hair on a whim? I think not.

Samson meditated on his invincibility; therefore, he never imagined that sharing his secret could harm him. Samson's assumption could have been harmless if he had surrounded himself with different people, but the combination of his associations and his meditative state of invincibility led to destructive consequences.

Judgment

The second factor which turned Samson's meditative state deadly was his judgment. Samson constantly underestimated the power, allegiances and intentions of the people around him. Samson had no idea that each time he went to sleep in Delilah's home she had men hidden, waiting to capture him. He was unaware of Delilah's hidden power. When a strong person underestimates the strength of a weak person, the strong person reveals his or her greatest weakness. Samson's meditative state, combined with his poor evaluation of Delilah's power, was a significant factor in his demise.

Regardless of how strong you are, if you do not have a healthy respect for the power that surrounds you, some form of harm is inevitable. One afternoon when I was cutting the grass, a detachable piece of the lawn mower fell off. Instead of cutting the mower off, I tried to attach the piece while it was still running. I almost lost two fingers because I did not respect the power of that machine. Each day we choose to put various foods in our bodies. When we underestimate the power that food has to destroy our bodies, we put ourselves at risk. When we nonchalantly view thousands of images, advertisements, movies and television shows, we open ourselves up to be influenced and manipulated in ways that compromise our wholeness and security. Similar to Samson, we underestimate the power of so many elements around us. As a result of those poor evaluations, so many of us are walking through the valley of death and do not even know it.

Delilah's Persistence

There was a third significant factor that helped to make Samson's meditative state harmful. Benjamin Franklin once said, "Energy and persistence conquer all things."[6] In the case of Samson, the energy and persistence of Delilah conquered him. Delilah persisted in her interrogation of Samson. She pushed, poked and prodded. Each time she pleaded to know his secret, Samson gave an inch. Those inches led to Samson's demise.

Samson's final nap with Delilah paralleled an insidious meditative state. Samson's time with Delilah was a steady crescendo, ending with him being put to sleep by Delilah.

Let us briefly examine each attempt Delilah makes to subdue Samson. In Delilah's first attempt to weaken Samson, Samson's sleep is implied. No word for sleep is ever used. Likewise, in Delilah's second attempt, Samson's sleep is not made explicit. In Delilah's third attempt, sleep (*shehah*) is explicitly mentioned. Once Delilah began to braid Samson's hair into a weaving loom, the author decided to clearly indicate that Samson was asleep.

When Samson finally divulged his secret to Delilah and Samson's hair was cut, the author became even more intentional in displaying Samson's sleep. The author used the word *yashen*, one of the words used to describe Adam's sleep in Genesis 2:21.

There seems to be a correlation between Samson's demise and the author's desire to show Samson sleeping. The closer Samson came to his demise, the more the author focused on

Samson's sleep. Yes, Samson's meditative posture on his invincibility was negative and unhealthy, but after Samson's last encounter with Delilah this meditative state made a fatal metamorphosis. One of the Philistines' first acts of vengeance was to take out Samson's eyes, which ironically symbolized the blindness he possessed to the people around him and his own shortcomings.

Samson's spiritual blindness caused him to miss much, particularly the proper associations and relationships to cultivate. For most of Samson's life he kept his natural eyes open and his spiritual eyes closed. There are some images, visions, insights that you will only be able to see with your spiritual eyes. So many of us go an entire lifetime without seeing what God has for us because we are afraid or unwilling to close our natural eyes and open our spiritual eyes.

When the Philistines impaired Samson physical sight, he showed signs of opening his spiritual eyes. Once his natural vision was taken, Samson acknowledged that he was weak without the Lord and could not afford to be forgotten by God.[7] This expression contrasts drastically with previous words and actions of invincibility (and a casual acknowledgement of God). Samson involuntarily lived out Jesus' saying that proclaimed, "If your right eye makes you stumble, tear it out and throw it from you; for it is better for you to lose one of the parts of your body, than for your whole body to be thrown into hell."[8] Samson's loss of sight led to a slightly greater godly perspective.

Like many people who took a few wrong turns in life, Samson had opportunities to escape his negative meditative state. His first opportunity to wake up came from his parents. If Samson had heeded his parents' advice and never pursued

Philistine women, then he would have never met Delilah, the facilitator of his demise.

Each day, week, month and year, we pass by little morsels of advice that can literally alter the course of our lives, but we label them as inconsequential. When I think back on all the times I have brushed off my parents' advice, I thank God all the more that there have been times when I have listened to them. As a result of embracing their advice, I was saved from many lives that would have been more difficult, less productive and less joyful.

Samson's story has a strong comic element to it. Every time Samson is with this woman, men are jumping out of nowhere, trying to capture him. One would think after a few times, Samson would make the connection between men trying to kill him and Delilah. One would think that after Samson had spent some time with Delilah, he would recognize that every date should not end with a battle. Maybe Samson had become so accustomed to dysfunctional relationships that he did not realize anything was wrong. For whatever the reason, Samson missed crucial cues that the scene he was in was a repeat and the ending would not be in his favor.

Conclusion

Samson is a prime example that all sleep stories do not have a happy ending. To stay in a negative meditative state for an extended time can often make a bad situation worse. Not waking up can result in serious consequences. It can cause us to miss out on so much: relationships, opportunities and new beginnings. Hopefully, we can all learn from Samson's mistakes.

Prayer

Gracious God, may we never believe that we are bigger than what we truly are. Remind us that you hold us in the palm of your hand. Encourage us to use the power we derived from you for your glory, not our own. Amen.

Reflection Questions

1) Has there ever been a time in your life when you thought you were invincible? What made you think that way?

2) What does misuse of divine power in the world look like? Give some modern examples.

3) How does God empower you?

Chapter 10
A Meditation of Self-Gratification

Mark 14:32-41

My wife and I have a very interesting morning routine. The night before, we discuss everything that we need to do and each place we must go. We set the alarm clock and go to sleep. The morning comes (always too quickly) and one of us arises almost immediately. We turn the alarm clock off and then run back to bed. For the next thirty to sixty minutes, we continue our sleep. We eventually take a glance at the clock, realize we are running late and go into overdrive to get ready. While we are preparing for our day, we lament about how we probably will not be able to accomplish all our desired goals or frequent all of our necessary places. We vow at that moment to get up earlier or at least on time. The next day comes and we start the pattern over again.

Even though my wife and I know where we need to go and what we must do, we allow the warmth of the covers, the softness of the pillows, and the heaviness of our eyelids to lure us back to bed. Our desire for comfort delays and sometimes prevents us from going to the places and accomplishing the tasks that are needed. I am certain our routine is common to many, because the desire for comfort is a trait we all share. We also share the negative repercussions that often come with the pursuit of comfort.

Peter, James and John could probably empathize with us. They experienced a similar situation in the garden of Gethsemane with Jesus. They desired to sleep and Jesus served as their irritating but needed alarm. Unfortunately, their meditative state of comfort overpowered the sound of Jesus' alarm.

Negative Meditation

In order to have a sense of the disciples' predicament at Gethsemane, we must first illuminate what precedes their sleep in the garden. The disciples and Jesus ate the Passover Feast and initiated the first communion meal. After they had become full from their food and wine, their natural inclination was probably to rest. Yet Jesus ushered them out of the house and just outside the city of Jerusalem to a place called Gethsemane. Jesus allowed all the disciples to relax with the exception of Peter, James and John. Jesus took the three a little further and commanded them to stay awake, while he advanced a bit further to pray.

Imagine Peter, James and John's situation. They had stomachs full of food. They had just traveled a little distance. They were taken to a garden. They were observing other people resting. Some reflection on rest and comfort was highly probable among them. The disciples' sleep in the garden represents more than just a physiological activity; it exposes their meditations on being comfortable. Barabara Holmes writes on the Gethsemane encounter in her book *Joy Unspeakable: Contemplative Practices of the Black Church*. She comments,

> In this periscope we see the difference between sleep and prayer, boundaries that are often blurred in the prayer life of a church focused on activity rather than repose. The disciples' response to Jesus' request that they contemplate and pray with him is not unlike our own. They begin and intend to abide with him, but they fall asleep...As the

language of Christian grace is co-opted to serve the needs of nationalism and consumerism, the church is warned to awaken from it lethargy. Only the discipline of contemplative practice will prepare us for the time of crisis when Jesus calls for the community of God to arise.[1]

Holmes highlights two important points. First, she identifies the association between sleep and "the prayer life", which includes the discipline of meditation. Second, she acknowledges the disciples' sleep as more than physiological but representative of a state of indolence. An association between sleep and an undesirable form of meditation is seen here.

Circumstances Disciples Cannot Overcome

Peter, James and John could not wake up from their meditative state because they could not overcome a few circumstances that confronted them at Gethsemane.

Reasonableness

The greatest circumstance that the disciples encountered was the reasonableness of their desire for sleep. They had legitimate reasons why they had fallen asleep and refrained from praying. They were tired. They had just finished eating. Everyone else was resting. It was the appropriate time for sleeping. Rationality was on their side, yet they were not on God's side.

If we are not careful, we can allow good reasons to be the demise of our spiritual life and even of the church itself. We have good reasons why we cannot go to church. We have good reasons why we cannot make commitments to serve. We have valid reasons why we cannot offer our financial support for

God's Kingdom. We have legitimate reasons why daily devotions for even 20 minutes are not practical. We have children to take to games. We have demanding, important jobs. We have family commitments and responsibilities that come first. We have hobbies that are necessary for our mental sanity. We need time to rest. We must sleep.

We have many justifiable reasons. Yet all the good reasons in the world do not automatically put us on God's side. The only thing that puts us on God's side is obedience. Grace can cover us no matter where we are, but obedience moves us to Christ's corner.

Sometimes God will desire that you take an action, even when you have a hundred and one good reasons not to do it. You may have plenty of good reasons why you should not pray for your enemy, but God says do it anyway. You may have plenty of bruises to show why you should not turn the other cheek, but God says do it anyway. You may have a lot of emotional scars to prove why you should not love your neighbor, but God says do it anyway. You may have plenty of obligations and responsibilities which validate why you should not be generous, but God says do it anyway. You may have plenty of important appointments to show why you cannot commit to service, but God says do it anyway. God says do it anyway and see what happens: just try it.

We live in a reason based society. We always want to know the reason why something should occur. But we have to be careful with reasons because reasons can always be created. You can find a reason for or against anything, but purposes are God-given. Sometimes we focus so much on the reason why something should or should not occur that we miss the God-given purpose. The reason why you are going into the hospital is to have surgery, but the purpose for you going into the hospital is to be a witness to a particular person. The reason why we have funerals is to say good bye to our love ones, but the purpose for a funeral is to remember that Christ conquered death. The reason why that relationship did not work is because of a clash in personalities, but the purpose behind it was so that you could grow closer to God. You can find a reason for anything you want. But instead of looking for a reason, start searching for God's purpose. Peter, James, and John had plenty of reasons of why they should go to sleep, but Jesus gave them a purpose for why they should stay awake. They had difficulty exiting their meditative state of comfort partly because they were entrapped by their own reasons.

Bare Side

The three disciples were also hindered by their inability to see Jesus' bare side. The language used to depict Jesus in the garden of Gethsemane was unique. The garden of Gethsemane account is the only instance where the gospel writers use words such as *ekthambeo* (distressed-NIV), *ademoneo* (troubled-NIV), and *perilypos* (sorrow-NIV) to describe Jesus' state. The disciples had been with Jesus for a few years and they had never seen him in that condition. Their leader, rabbi, counselor, advisor and savior seemed so vulnerable. That probably terrified the disciples. They had no idea what to do because they were in uncharted territory.

One of the scariest moments of my life was when I first saw my mother break down and cry. My father had suffered a massive stroke. We did not know if he would make it out of the hospital. The doctors said his chances of survival were limited. After coming from the hospital, I looked at my mother and saw her face turn red. She burst into tears. As her head lowered, I stood there in utter shock. I did not know what to say or do. I could not believe that any situation would impact her so adversely. She was always so strong, dependable and together. Her vulnerability and fear made me feel vulnerable and fearful because she was my protector.

Peter, James and John are often described as Jesus' inner circle. Jesus consistently singled them out to go a few places and see a few things that other disciples were not privy to. One could speculate that Jesus felt closer to these three. He may have felt that they grasped more fully what he was about. If Jesus was going to be bare, let his guard down, be exposed and vulnerable around anyone, then these three disciples were probably his best options. However, Peter, James and John could not handle the responsibility of seeing their leader in such a state. The disciples attempted to escape the situation through sleep.

When Jesus took Peter, James and John up a mountain and exposed them to his glory, in an event known as the transfiguration, they had no problem embracing the moment. They wanted to capture the moment. They wanted to see as much of God's glory as they could. They wanted to hear as much of the conversation between Elijah, Moses and Jesus as they could. They wanted to savor and remember their time on the mountain with Jesus. When Jesus pulled them aside to experience a different type of intimacy with him, they did not show the same enthusiasm and interest.

We so freely receive from God. We easily accept all the blessings that come from an intimate relationship with Christ. Yet when our intimacy calls for more devotion time, undesirable service in the community, or commitment to a ministry in the church, we often become a lot more reluctant.

Any intimate relationship with Christ is going to involve experiencing a bare side. You will encounter situations that are not always pleasant because of your intimate relationship with Christ. You will partake in activities that are not always enjoyable and easy because of your intimate relationship with Christ. Similar to marriage, intimacy with Christ brings about wonderful experiences and benefits, but it also brings some things that are untidy and difficult to handle.

The church has a bare (some would even say an ugly) side. There are aspects of the church that are not pleasant. Conflict resolution, financing ministry initiatives, balancing tradition with innovation or trying to meet diverse needs are not pleasant, joyous experiences, but Christians must deal with them to be the Body of Christ to the world. Those who are willing to deal with the less glamorous aspects of the Church are always the ones who are the most spiritually mature. Peter, James and John wanted to have their cake and eat it. The three disciples had no problem reaping the benefits of being in Jesus' inner circle, but were not willing to exit their comfort zone to accept the sacrifices that came from being in that same circle.

Self-Monitor

The three disciples' inability to monitor themselves also hindered them from exiting their meditative state of comfort. Jesus left them and expected that they would be mature enough to follow his orders. He did not stay and hold their hands. He did not look over their shoulders. He did not micromanage them. Jesus wanted the disciples to be capable to follow orders without his supervision. The disciples did not live up to Christ's desire.

The followers of Jesus often faded in their intensity or effort when Jesus' physical presence left them. When Peter was around Jesus, he had no problem telling everyone that Jesus was the Messiah. Yet when Jesus was arrested, Peter denied that he knew Jesus. When the 10 lepers were around Jesus, they had no problem begging for mercy. Yet when they left Jesus and were healed, nine of them did not give Jesus another call. When the sisters, Mary and Martha, were in Jesus' presence, they were hopeful. Yet when the sisters were separated from Jesus by a few towns and their brother died, they stopped believing in Jesus' healing power. The disciples were confident and focused on their mission when Jesus was eating with them and teaching them. Yet when Jesus was put on the cross, they lost their sense of direction and scattered.

Do you need signs of Jesus' physical presence in order to execute a life of faith? Do you need to be in church, or to be with a fellow Christian, or to have someone watching you for you to act as a person of faith?

My health insurance company recently started a disease prevention program. We are assigned a health coach. The coach calls you every six to eight weeks and asks you very blunt questions about your diet, exercise routine, weight and other pertinent information. The coach has encouraged me to cut down on carbohydrates, increase my physical activity and make sure that I am maintaining a healthy weight, just to name a few suggestions. Ninety percent of everything my health coach told me, I already knew. I did not start enacting many of the things I knew until she started holding me accountable.

As a result of someone monitoring my health on a consistent basis, I was forced to do what I already should have been doing. I will never become a healthy person (in a holistic sense) until I can recognize and apply healthy lifestyle practices without continual prompting. A healthy person does not exercise or maintain a certain diet because someone constantly reminds her or him. Likewise, a person of faith does not pray, believe, fast or practice any other type of spiritual discipline because someone tells her or him to do so. They pray, believe, fast or practice spiritual disciplines because they have recognized the value of that lifestyle for themselves and have chosen to live by it. The disciples did not get it. They did not get what being a person of faith was all about. They still needed to be monitored. They needed to be watched over. They needed to be managed. Their need for supervision hindered them from exiting their meditative state of comfort.

Conclusion

One of the top causes for the decline and irrelevancy of so many churches is the desire to be comfortable. More specifically, it is the meditative state of comfort. Church members get caught in a mindset of continually reflecting on questions such as "How can this building benefit us?" "How can this worship experience be more enjoyable to us?" "What type of music is pleasant to our ears?" "What types of activities work for us?" and "What makes us comfortable?" Focusing on these questions will be the death of the church.

I served on the board of a food assistance organization founded and supported by a coalition of churches. The organization was going through a time of transition because many of the original members had died, moved away or were no longer able to help. In response, we began to look for new ways to effectively meet our current challenges and serve our constituency (the working poor).

After months of deliberation, a few board members suggested that we could begin providing food assistance on Saturday. This would allow us to pull from a greater pool of volunteers and would make our services available to a greater number of people. When we agreed to open on Saturday, the sole paid employee of the organization stated, "I don't want to work on Saturdays."

Her one statement captured poignantly why so many churches will "go out of business." Whenever the employees' comfort takes precedent over the customers' comfort, the company will not stay in business long.

As followers of Christ, our "customers" are not the people inside the church, but the people outside the church—the lost and unsaved. Those are the people that we must be reaching out to and catering to in order to stay in the business of making disciples for Jesus Christ. The church was created for the very people who have yet to enter. If we do not break our meditative state of comfort, a collapse of many churches is inevitable. Let us never be too comfortable to prevent the building up of God's kingdom on Earth.

Prayer

Blessed Savior, what makes us comfortable can also make us weak and inflexible. You do not call us to be comfortable, but to be faithful. You do not desire that our every whim and preference is addressed, but that we serve others. Breathe into us and on us. Awaken us from our sleep. Amen.

Reflection Questions

1) What distinguishes healthy comfort from unhealthy comfort for you?

2) Reflect on a time when God has called you to be uncomfortable. Why do you think God was calling you to do that? What were the results?

3) In what way has your faith community become comfortable from an unhealthy perspective? How can you assist in addressing this constructively?

Chapter 11
A Meditation of Will

1 Samuel 26:5-7, 12

My barber and I have this ongoing debate about God. He says that if God already knows our futures, then our fates are determined (because what God knows cannot be wrong). I respond by saying God's knowledge does not preclude our free will. We go back and forth for a few rounds—repeating the same point over again. We then switch the topic out of utter frustration. We both believe the other does not get it.

To be all-knowing is a powerful asset, but I do not believe it forces me to act. My mother would often tell me when I was young that she knew me better than I knew myself. She could anticipate certain reactions that I would make. She could sense when I was upset and why. She could predict what would make me happy and what would make me sad. She never forced me to react in a certain way, to be happy, to be sad or to be upset, but she still had a good sense of what I would do.

I was raised in a Christian tradition that taught free will. The idea that I had a choice to do right or wrong, to go left or right, to speak or not to speak, to be obedient or disobedient was a notion as fundamental to me as the notion of gravity. I rarely encountered anyone who believed otherwise. Quite frankly, I would not have even known if I met someone that believed differently, because I would have just assumed that they believed in free will also. Does anyone really believe that we have no control or say over the direction of our lives? Maybe my American, middle class, upwardly mobile mentality has clouded my vision, but a life that is already set is not worth living. A script that cannot be altered is not worth performing.

Yet I think what my barber was alluding to was something much bigger than fatalism. Even in a world where individual free will is affirmed and practiced, the inevitability of God's way seems to loom. God knows what will occur, and maybe our free will can impact how and when it will occur. I believe that there is a tension between our free will and God's will.

God will allow us to try as many detours as we have the energy to take, but in the end, she knows that her way is best. The will of God is subtle, persistent and eternal, and it will outlast any desire or decision we could ever make. Some choose to fight against it, to speak over it, to control and decide in spite of it, but in the end, can anyone resist it?

I often tell my Bible class that we have a fundamental choice to swim with the current of God's *logos* (way) or to swim against it. Regardless of how we choose to swim, God's current will keep on going. We all have seen it: a person who simply made the same mistake over and over, whether in relationships, finances, family affairs or whatever. Those people in certain aspects of their life simply do not get it. They are always swimming against God's current. Peace and resolution will not emerge until they start going with God's flow.

Negative Meditation

An examination of Saul's life reveals that a meditative life on having it our way will lead to our demise. Saul was a control freak. He consistently tried to impose his will on a situation rather than try to become one with God's will. When the prophet Samuel did not come in the anticipated time to offer a sacrifice, Saul decided to perform the sacrifice himself.[1] He was unable to wait in God's mysterious time, but decided that meeting a deadline was more important. When Saul and the Israelite army went to battle, Saul commanded his soldiers not to eat during the day until he secured his vengeance.[2] The army stopped their normal diet for the sake of Saul's ambitions. When David agreed to fight Goliath, Saul tried to control the materials (and therefore the methods) that David was accustomed to fighting with.[3] When Saul believed David was a threat to his throne, he tried to prevent David from ascending by killing him.[4] Saul's life reveals a pattern of trying to force his will, desires and ambitions unto a situation, thereby neglecting the current of God.

Saul's meditative state is crystallized in 1st Samuel 26:7. Saul sought to capture David. He became consumed with controlling David's life to preserve his legacy and rule. In the context of this pursuit and these obsessive reflections, Saul slept. The context of Saul's sleep is similar to the type of meditation that consumed him. There was a spear placed into the ground beside Saul's head as he slept. Saul's spear was a significant instrument because it was the weapon with which he consistently tried to eliminate his inevitable successor: David. While David was playing the harp in the palace, Saul tried to assassinate him with a spear two times.[5] Saul threw a spear at his own son, Jonathan, because he defended David.[6] The spear was an instrument that Saul used to control his own fate. He used it to ensure the continuation of his royal dynasty. Saul sleeping beside the spear captured the meditative state in which he was entangled, a state focused on his will.

Saul is initially depicted as being in a state of sleep (*shakab*). Our passage ends by describing Saul in a trancelike state in verse twelve (*tardemah*). God placed Saul in this last state as a way to protect David while he moved among Saul and his army. Saul's will was eventually overpowered by God's will, but not as a result of God forcing Saul to do something. Saul chose to enter into a meditative state. God simply took Saul's meditative state and turned it into a trance (deep sleep), so Saul would not harm David. Saul chose to use his spear as a way to preserve his dynasty, but he ended up using his spear to try to take his own life.[7]

Many people of faith have a conception of prayer that is out of sync with the Scriptures. When I conduct workshops on prayer at churches, I often begin by asking the group for their definitions of prayer. Most people respond by defining prayer as talking to God or communicating with God in some form. The definitions always include references to having one's request granted and being heard by God. Yet one of the most fundamental aspects of prayer is always overlooked: the search for God's will. Jesus told his disciples, "This, then, is how you should pray: Our Father in heaven, hallowed be your name, your kingdom come, your will be done on Earth as it is in heaven..."[8] Jesus taught his disciples that an essential component of prayer is aligning oneself with God's will. Jesus not only taught this message, but practiced it. Before Jesus' death in the garden of Gethsemane, he prays, "My Father, if it is possible, may this cup be taken from me. Yet not as I will, but as you will."[9] Jesus expressed his desire, but ended his prayer by yielding to God's will. Prayer is a process that involves the alignment of our will with God's will. If Saul would have prayed, his fate could have been different.

Conclusion

What would happen if more Christians stop simply talking to God and start to pray? What would happen if more Christians stop simply making requests to God and start to pray? What would happen if more Christians stop simply communicating and expressing themselves to God and start to pray? Yes, prayer does change things because God's will on Earth changes things. Whenever we pray (as defined from a biblical perspective) we are beginning the process of aligning our wills with God's will and thereby beginning the process of making earth "as it is in heaven." The interaction between God's will and our will is an interesting combination. It is something we probably will never fully understand while on Earth. Yet I am sure of one thing: alignment with God's will is the best place to be.

Prayer

Holy Spirit, may we eagerly surrender to your will. Show us all the fruits that can come from being aligned with you. May your ways become our ways and your thoughts become our thoughts. Amen.

Reflection Questions

1) What do you desire more than anything else? Why? Where does that desire come from?

2) Reflect on a time when your desires came back to harm you. Why do you think this occurred?

3) If God's will was the only will that existed, what would this world look like? How would this world be different (i.e., your job, school, neighborhood, church, country, gym, etc.)?

Conclusion

There are parts of God's presence that are murky, uncertain and difficult to see and experience. There are parts of God's presence that are dark! When we approach the edges of God's darkness, those are the moments when we must choose if we are going to trust him. They are the moments when we must meditate.

When Adam was in the darkness of God and had no idea of who would be compatible for him, he slept. During his sleep, an aspect of himself was given up so that he could be in a healthy union with another. When Abram was in the darkness of God and did not know when God was going to deliver on his promise, Abram slept. During his sleep, he remained still and received insight about his future.

Just as the darkness of God leads us to meditate, the light of God awakens us out of destructive meditative states. The light of God shined on Jairus' daughter and she awoke out of her lifeless meditative state. The light of God shined on Eutchyus and he awoke out of his harmful state. The light of God shined on Jonah and he awoke out of his stubbornness. The light of God is capable of awakening us out of meditative slumbers.

A few find themselves in a twilight zone, suspended between darkness and light. They do not surrender to the darkness of God and meditate on the things of God. Neither do they allow the light of God to penetrate their negative meditative states. Instead they decide to wallow in their own darkness and be led by their own illumination.

Samson remained in his own darkness. He was oblivious to the advice of his elders. He never allowed the light of God to wake him up. The disciples remained in their own darkness. They focused on all the benefits of comfort while missing the pleasures of sacrifice. They never allowed the light of Christ to wake them up. Saul remained in his own darkness. His obsession with control clouded everything he saw. He never allowed the light of God to wake him up.

Are your ready to sleep with God every night and awake with him every morning? A one night stand will not do. Are you ready to have a truly intimate relationship with God that surpasses your wildest dreams and your most fanciful pleasures? Are you ready to take that "next step" in your relationship?

I pray the scandal has started in your church by now. I pray that the gossip lines are flooded with the news. I pray that the people in the community are starting to drive by your church and whisper to one another. I pray that all the rumors may be even more salacious than others first heard. Lastly, I pray that all who hear about it and all who talk about it may join in and experience the scandal firsthand for themselves.

Endnotes

Note to Reader

[1] Acts 20:7.

[2] Acts 5:42.

[3] Acts 9:18-19, 16:31-32.

[4] Exodus 3:5.

[5] Matthew 2:11, NASB.

[6] Matthew 4:9.

[7] Matthew 20:20.

[8] Psalm 119:15.

Preface

[9] Cynthia Bourgeault, *Centering Prayer and Inner Awakening* (Maryland: Cowley Publications, 2004), 59.

[10] Peter Toon, *From Mind to Heart: Christian Meditation Today* (Michigan: Baker Book House, 1987), 35.

Introduction

[1] Thomas H. McAlpine, *Sleep, Divine & Human, in the Old Testament* (England: Sheffield Press, 1987), 15.

[2] Robert Bailey, "Is 'Sleep' the Proper Biblical Term for the Intermediate State?" *Zietschrift fur die Neutestamentliche Wissenschaft* 55, no. 3-4 (1964): 161-167.

[3] Genesis 26:10, New International Version.

[4] NIV.

[5] Ibid.

[6] Psalm 121:4-5 NIV.

[7] Bernard Batto, "When God Sleeps." *Bible Review* 3, no. 4 (1987): 22.

[8] Isaiah 29:10-11a, NIV.

[9] Mark 13:32-37, NIV.

[10] Thomas Thomas, "The Meaning of 'Sleep' in 1 Thessalonians 5:10." *Journal of Evangelical Theological.*

Society 22, no. 4 (1979): 345-349.

[11] Psalm 13:3, NIV.

[12] NIV.

[13] 1 Corinthians 15:51-52, NIV.

[14] Matthew 27:52, King James Version.

[15] McAlpine, 42-43.

[16] Ibid.

[17] NIV.

[18] Ibid.

[19] Genesis 24:63, NIV.

[20] NIV.

[21] Peter Toon, *The Art of Meditating on Scripture* (Michigan: Zondervan Publishing, 1993), 23.

[22] Ibid, 24.

[23] Psalm 4:4, NKJV.

[24] St. Athanasius, *St. Athanasius: Life of St. Anthony* (ebook, 2010), location 663 of 1103.

[25] John Cassian, *Conferences of John Cassian* (New Century Books, 2010) location 5168 of 10748.

[26] James Finely provides a clear and concise explanation of the relationship between meditation and contemplation in Chapter 1 of his book *Christian Meditation* (Harper Collins, 2008).

[27] William Johnston, ed., *The Cloud of Unknowing & The Book of Privy Counseling* (New York: Doubleday, 2005), 155.

[28] Ibid, 29.

[29] Richard Foster, *Celebration of Discipline-25ᵗʰ Anniversary* (Harper Collins e-books, 2004) location 4884 of 5901.

[30] Comparative Study Bible (Michigan: Zondervan, 1999) Matthew 1:20, 24, KJV.

[31] Matthew 27:46, NKJV.

[32] John 6:15b-17, NKJV.

[33] Luke 11:1-4.

[34] Luke 9:28-32, Mark 14:32-42.

[35] NKJV.

[36] Ibid.

[37] Ibid.

[38] Thomas Merton, *Spiritual Direction & Meditation* (Minnesota: Liturgical Press, 1960), 52.

[39] John Woodbridge, ed., *Renewing Your Mind in a Secular World* (Chicago: Moody Press, 1985), 43.

[40] NKJ.

[41] Ibid.

Chapter 1 Missing Rib Meditation

[1] Matthew 22:37-38, NIV.

[2] Genesis 2:18 NIV.

[3] Stephen Renn, ed., *Expository Dictionary of Bible Words* (Massachusetts: Hendrickson, 2005), 443.

[4] Robert K. Barnhart, ed., *Chambers Dictionary of Etymology* (New York: Chambers, 1988), 498.

[5] NIV.

[6] NIV.

[7] Ibid., NIV.

[8] Ephesians 2:2, NIV.

[9] See Genesis 4:8.

[10] Ibid. Genesis 37:14-20.

[11] See 1st Samuel 16:9-11.

[12] See Acts 1:18.

[13] Matthew 16:25, NIV.

[14] Matthew 16:23.

[15] Matthew 16:20.

[16] Matthew 16:21.

[17] Matthew 7:14.

[18] Luke 19:9.

[19] Emerito Nacpil & Douglas Elwood, ed., *The Human and the Holy* (New York: Orbis, 1980), 41.

[20] See Mark 8:31 and John 3:16.

How to Sleep with God

[1] Luke 23:45, NIV.

Chapter 2 Seer Meditation

[1] See Exodus 33:12-13.

[2] See 2nd Kings 6:15-17.

[3] See Acts 9:1-7.

[4] See Matthew 28:1-9.

[5] Genesis 15:6.

[6] Mark 9:24.

[7] Genesis 15:9, NIV.

[8] NIV.

[9] Exodus 3:2

[10] Exodus 13:22.

[11] Acts 2:3.

[12] I Kings 18:38.

How to Sleep with God

[1] Genesis 1:3 NIV.

Chapter 3 Rocking Boat meditation

[1] Matthew 3:17 NIV.

[2] See Easter 6:1.

[3] See Daniel 6:18.

[4] See John 8:7-11.

[5] See Matthew 15:22-28.

[6] See Matthew 26:51-53.

[7] Matthew 8:28 mentions two demon possessed men.

[8] NIV.

[9] Mark 5:6, NIV.

How to Sleep with God

[1] Mark 4:39, KJV.

Chapter 4 Conscious Meditation

[2] Matthew 8:20, NKJV.

Chapter 5 Walking Dead Reverse Meditation

[1] See Mark 5:21-34.

[2] Mark 5:33-34, KJV

[3] See Mark 2:4-11.

[4] Mark 2:9, NKJ.

[5] John 6:48, NIV.

[6] John 11:25, NIV.

[7] John 1:4, NIV.

[8] John 6:22-40

[9] Mk 6:5-6, NKJ.

[10] Luke 23:39-43.

[11] Matthew 8:3, NIV.

[12] Matthew 8:15, NIV.

[13] Mark 16:18, NIV.

Chapter 6 Church Reverse Meditation

[1] See 2nd Kings 2:23-24.

[2] See Numbers 22:21-31.

[3] See Genesis Ch 3.

[4] 1st Corinthians 11:20-22a, NIV.

[5] Matthew 14:16, NIV.

[6] KJV.

[7] NIV.

[8] New American Standard Bible.

[9] Alfred Marshall, trans., *The Interlinear NASB-NIV Parallel New Testament in Greek and English* (Michigan: Zondervan, 1993), 408.

[10] John Kohlenberg and James Swanson, editors, *The Strongest Strong's Concordance* (Michigan: Zondervan, 2001), 1601.

[11] Ibid., 409.

[12] Stephen Renn, ed., *Expository Dictionary of Bible Words* (Massachusetts: Hendrickson, 2005), 956.

[13] See Luke 24:13-35.

Chapter 7 Escape Reverse Meditation

[1] Jonah 1:9, NIV.

[2] Jonah 1:17, NIV.

[3] See Genesis 41:7.

[4] See Exodus 7:12.

[5] See Numbers 16:32.

Chapter 8 Fate Reverse Meditation

[1] John 6:34-35.

[2] Matthew 13:58.

[3] John 20:25.

[4] Luke 23:39.

[5] Acts 12:5, KJV.

[6] Matthew 24:42-44, NASB.

[7] Craig Lambert, "Facial Pheenoms." Harvard Magazine, September-October 2009, 7-8.

Chapter 9 A Meditation of Invincibility

[1] See Judges 13:5.

[2] Ibid.

[3] See Judges 15:15-17 and 16:3.

[4] NASB.

[5] See Judges 16:17.

[6] http://www.quotationspage.com/quotes/Benjamin_Franklin/.

[7] Judges 16:28.

[8] Matthew 5:29, NASB.

Chapter 10 A Meditation of Self-Gratification

[1] Barbara Ann Holmes, *Joy Unspeakable: Contemplative Practices of the Black Church* (Minneapolis, Ausburg Fortress: 2004), 133- 134.

Chapter 11 A Meditation of Will

[1] See 1st Samuel 13:8-12.

[2] See 1st Samuel 14:24.

[3] See 1st Samuel 17:38-39.

4 See 1st Samuel 18:11.

5 See 1st Samuel 18:10-11 and 1 Sam. 19:9-10.

6 See 1st Samuel 20:33.

7 See 2nd Samuel 1:16.

8 Matthew 6:9-10, NIV.

9 Matthew 26:39, NIV.

CPSIA information can be obtained at www.ICGtesting.com
Printed in the USA
BVOW031559091211

277737BV00006B/10/P